Irish Chain
QUILTS

Contemporary Twists on a Classic Design

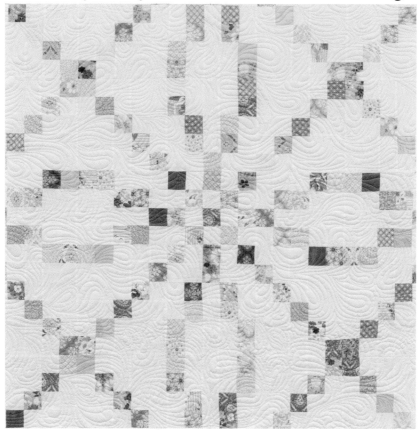

Melissa Corry

Martingale®
Create with Confidence

Dedication

TO MY FAMILY

Irish Chain Quilts:
Contemporary Twists on a Classic Design
© 2015 by Melissa Corry

Martingale®
19021 120th Ave. NE, Ste. 102
Bothell, WA 98011-9511 USA
ShopMartingale.com

Printed in China
20 19 18 17 16 15   8 7 6 5 4 3 2 1

Library of Congress Cataloging-in-Publication Data is available upon request.

ISBN: 978-1-60468-555-8

Mission Statement

Dedicated to providing quality products and service to inspire creativity.

Credits

PUBLISHER AND CHIEF VISIONARY OFFICER
Jennifer Erbe Keltner

EDITORIAL DIRECTOR	DESIGN DIRECTOR
Karen Costello Soltys	Paula Schlosser
ACQUISITIONS EDITOR	PHOTOGRAPHER
Karen M. Burns	Brent Kane
TECHNICAL EDITOR	PRODUCTION MANAGER
Ellen Pahl	Regina Girard
COPY EDITOR	COVER AND INTERIOR DESIGNER
Melissa Bryan	Connor Chin
	ILLUSTRATOR
	Lisa Lauch

What's your creative passion?

Find it at **ShopMartingale.com**

books • eBooks • ePatterns • daily blog • free projects
videos • tutorials • inspiration • giveaways

Contents

Introduction

As her wedding gift for my husband and me, my mother made us a beautiful queen-size Double Irish Chain quilt. It was done in solid greens and cream and was our master bedspread for many years. As some of my children reached the toddler age, it became a little "well loved" and was moved to a quilt rack to be admired. This was one of the first quilts my mother ever made, and it will always be a treasured heirloom.

The Double Irish Chain wedding quilt created by my mother and cherished by my entire family

As I get to know so many wonderful quilting friends through teaching and the online community, I often find myself smiling inwardly when I hear about quilters who began their quiltmaking journey with the influence of an Irish Chain. It seems to be a wonderful starting place for so many who fall in love with quilting.

And why shouldn't it be? The Irish Chain, a rich traditional design dating back to Colonial times, is universally known for its wonderful movement,

> *An Irish Chain seems to be a wonderful starting place for those who fall in love with quilting.*

> "I've often found myself playing with the traditional crisscross design of the Irish Chain."

ease of piecing, and elegant collaboration of color. As my initial introduction to quilting involved a beautiful Irish Chain, it's no surprise that this design has always been special to me.

Because of that special love, I have often found myself playing with the traditional crisscross design of the Irish Chain. I created a few tutorials and patterns using variations, and found that I loved the Irish Chain more and more as I transformed it into new and exciting designs. I hope to share that love through this book and open a whole new world of Irish Chain designs for quilters of today. The designs all have a common theme but are as different and individual as the fabrics from which they're made.

I don't define myself as a particular type of quilter. I love designs of all sorts. Some days I feel like tossing all the rules out the window and throwing together fabrics without a plan. Other days I want lots of precise cutting, followed by a wonderfully therapeutic session of chain piecing. I love creating and being allowed to jump from one type of design to another. It keeps each quilting day interesting and helps push me out of my design comfort zone.

Because I like diversity, this book is divided into four parts: Twist on Tradition, Modern Patchwork, Improvisational Piecing, and Appliquéd Chains. Each category features quilts in varying sizes that blend the traditional Irish

Chain crisscross design with contemporary concepts. So now, you too can easily jump from one type of design to another.

This book was created for all quilters who, like me, love the Irish Chain. Maybe it was your introduction to quilting, and I encourage you to keep it with you on your quilting journey as much today as ever. I hope you love these wonderful designs and find them to be fun to make and even more fun to love. I also hope you expand your quilting boundaries by trying projects from each of the four categories and breaking out of your quilting comfort zone. But most of all, I hope that you find joy in your quiltmaking journey.

Thank you for taking part in this dream come true.

Happy quilting!
Melissa

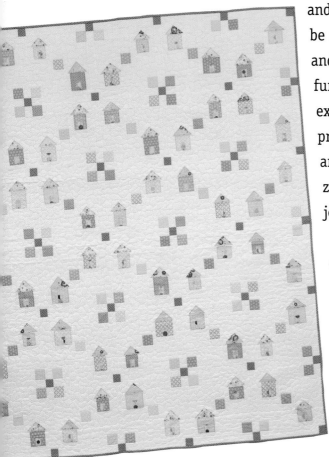

> *The designs all have a common theme, but are as different and individual as the fabrics from which they're made.*

Twist on Tradition

I love designing traditional quilts with a modern twist. Just what do I mean by that? Pretty simply, it's just what it sounds like—a mixture of traditional elements with a modern twist. This can be as simple as using more-modern fabrics, changing the scale of a block, or modifying the block arrangement. These "modern traditional quilts" preserve tried-and-true patterns but show them in a fresh new way.

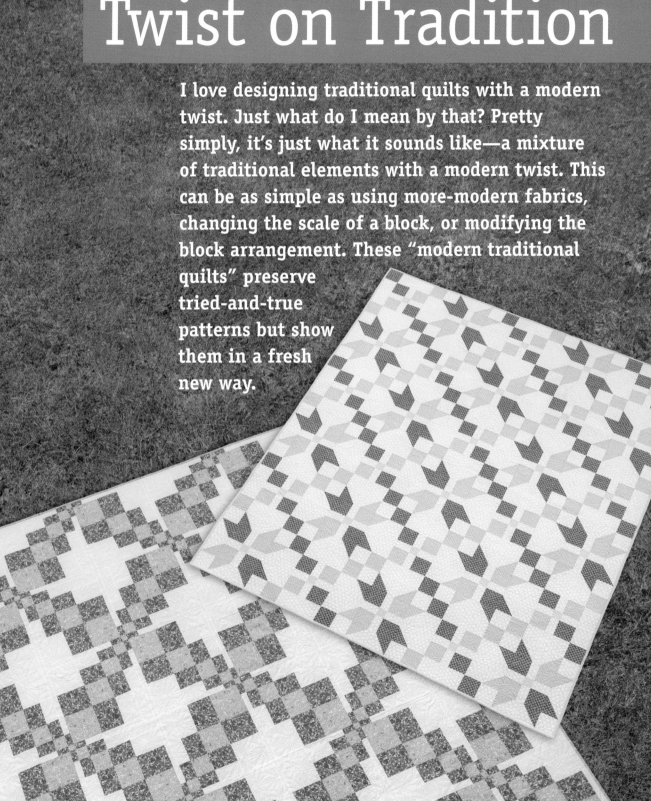

Breaking Up

"Breaking Up," designed and made by Melissa Corry.
Fabrics are Vintage Verona by Emily Taylor Design for Riley Blake Designs.

This fun design includes squares in alternating sizes, "breaking up" the chain of smaller squares. This quilt was the turning point for me—when I made the leap from pondering to pursuing a book of Irish Chain projects.

Finished quilt:
56½" x 74½",
lap size

Finished block:
16" x 16"

Materials

Yardage is based on 42"-wide fabric.

3¼ yards of white solid for block backgrounds

1 yard *total* of assorted prints for blocks

⅝ yard of navy solid for blocks

⅝ yard of fabric for binding

3⅔ yards of fabric for backing

66" x 84" piece of batting

Add Variety

Using precuts is a great way to add lots of variety in your quilt. "Breaking Up" is 5"-square or charm-pack friendly. So grab a stack or two of squares and start cutting.

Cutting

From the navy solid, cut:

6 strips, 2½" x 42"

From the white solid, cut:

3 strips, 6½" x 42"

9 strips, 2½" x 42"; crosscut *6 strips* into 48 rectangles, 2½" x 4½"

6 strips, 4½" x 42"; crosscut into 48 squares, 4½" x 4½"

2 strips, 16½" x 42"; crosscut into 31 rectangles, 2½" x 16½"

From the assorted prints, cut:

48 squares, 4½" x 4½"

20 squares, 2½" x 2½"

From the binding fabric, cut:

7 strips, 2½" x 42"

Piecing the A Blocks

1 Referring to "Strip Piecing" on page 74, sew a navy 2½" x 42" strip and a white 6½" x 42" strip together as shown. Press the seam allowances toward the navy strip. Make three strip sets. Cut 48 segments, 2½" wide.

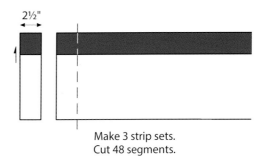

2½"

Make 3 strip sets.
Cut 48 segments.

2 Sew two white 2½" x 4½" rectangles and one print 4½" square together as shown. Press the seam allowances toward the print square. Make 24 units.

Make 24.

The Details

When I began to plan the machine quilting for this quilt, I quickly realized that I would have to use more than one thread color. Using white thread in the navy and print fabrics would have stood out too much. It's a bit more time consuming, but it's worth the extra time to switch threads. When using more than one thread color, always start with the color that will cover the most space, usually the background, and quilt everything with that color. Then go back and quilt with the second color in the remaining areas—in this case the chains.

3 Pin and sew segments from step 1 to opposite sides of a unit from step 2 to complete block A. Press the seam allowances open. Make 24 blocks.

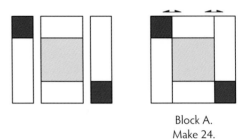

Block A.
Make 24.

Piecing the B Blocks

1 Sew a navy 2½" x 42" strip and a white 2½" x 42" strip together lengthwise. Press the seam allowances toward the navy strip. Make three strip sets. Cut 48 segments, 2½" wide.

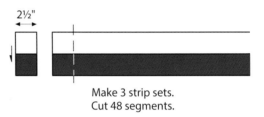

Make 3 strip sets.
Cut 48 segments.

2 Pin and sew two segments together, rotating them as shown to make a four-patch unit. Press the seam allowances open. Make 24 four-patch units.

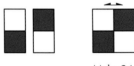

Make 24.

3 Pin and sew one four-patch unit, two white 4½" squares, and one print 4½" square together to make block B. Press the seam allowances as indicated by the arrows. Make 24 blocks.

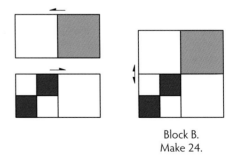

Block B.
Make 24.

Piecing the AB Blocks

Lay out two A blocks and two B blocks as shown. Sew the blocks together into rows and press the seam allowances open. Pin and sew the rows together. Press the seam allowances open. Make 12 of block AB.

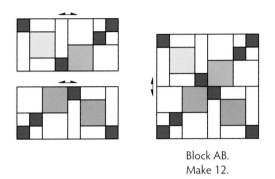

Block AB.
Make 12.

Assembling the Quilt Top

1 Lay out the AB blocks in four rows with three blocks per row, rotating the blocks as shown in the assembly diagram at right. Add the white 2½" x 16½" rectangles and the print 2½" squares around the blocks to create the sashing.

2 Sew the sashing rectangles and print squares into rows. Press the seam allowances toward the sashing rectangles. Pin and sew the sashing rectangles and AB blocks into rows. Press the seam allowances toward the sashing rectangles.

Balancing the Layout

The corner squares in the sashing are a great help when it comes to balancing the color distribution in your quilt top. Spend some time arranging and rearranging the blocks and corner squares until you are completely satisfied with the arrangement of the assorted prints.

3 Pin and sew the rows together, finishing the quilt top. Press the seam allowances open.

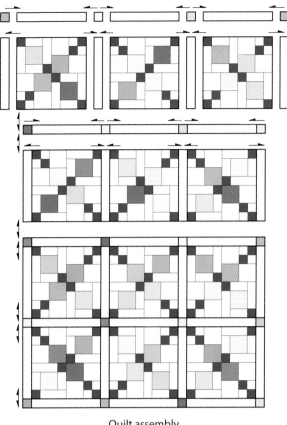

Quilt assembly

Finishing the Quilt

1 Cut the backing fabric in half to create two 66"-long pieces. Remove the selvages and sew the two halves together using a ½" seam allowance; press the seam allowances to one side. Trim the backing to approximately 66" x 84".

2 Layer the backing, batting, and quilt top. Baste the three layers together using your preferred method.

3 Quilt as desired. I used a traveling curl throughout the background and echo quilted arches in the print and navy fabrics.

4 Referring to "Binding a Quilt" on page 77, bind your quilt using the 2½"-wide strips.

Two Paths Crossed

"Two Paths Crossed," designed and made by Melissa Corry.
Fabrics are April Showers by Bonnie and Camille for Moda.

Adding what appears to be sashing through the center of a traditional star block creates a design with a wonderful modern twist and lots of movement. The resulting interplay between the star block and the chain block makes the stars seem to dance over the quilt top. This design includes a lucky bonus—it's mainly strip pieced, so it will go together in a snap.

Finished quilt:
68" x 81½",
twin size

Finished block:
13½" x 13½"

Materials

Yardage is based on 42"-wide fabric.

3⅞ yards of white polka dot for block backgrounds

1⅜ yards of navy print for blocks

1⅜ yards of lime-green print for blocks

¼ yard of yellow print for blocks*

⅔ yard of fabric for binding*

5 yards of fabric for backing

78" x 91" piece of batting

If you wish to bind the quilt with the same yellow print as for blocks, you'll need a total of ⅞ yard.

Cutting

From the white polka dot, cut:
3 strips, 8" x 42"
19 strips, 3½" x 42"; crosscut 15 strips into:
    30 rectangles, 3½" x 8"
    60 squares, 3½" x 3½"
    60 rectangles, 2" x 3½"
6 strips, 2" x 42"
6 strips, 4" x 42"; crosscut into 60 squares,
    4" x 4"

From the yellow print, cut:
2 strips, 2" x 42"

From the navy print, cut:
9 strips, 3½" x 42"
3 strips, 4" x 42"; crosscut into 30 squares,
    4" x 4"

From the lime-green print, cut:
9 strips, 3½" x 42"
3 strips, 4" x 42"; crosscut into 30 squares,
    4" x 4"

From the binding fabric, cut:
8 strips, 2½" x 42"

Piecing the Block Centers

1 Referring to "Strip Piecing" on page 74, sew a white 3½" x 42" strip to each side of a yellow 2" x 42" strip to make a strip set. Press the seam allowances toward the yellow strip. Make two strip sets. Cut 30 segments, 2" wide.

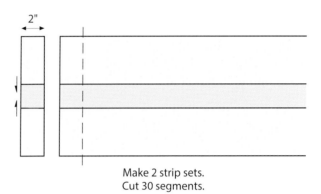

Make 2 strip sets.
Cut 30 segments.

2 Sew a navy 3½" x 42" strip, a white 2" x 42" strip, and a lime-green 3½" x 42" strip together to make a strip set. Press the seam allowances toward the navy and green prints. Make six strip sets. Cut 60 segments, 3½" wide.

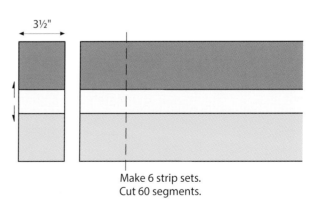

Make 6 strip sets.
Cut 60 segments.

The Details

When piecing the units of this quilt, pay close attention to the positioning of your colors and the direction of your units. It's very easy to mix up the placement of this quilt and you don't realize it until you have a star sewn together with a backward point (speaking from experience). I find it helps to place the half-square triangles and squares on my mat the same way I'll be sewing them. Then I can match them up and take them right to the machine and know I haven't inadvertently spun them.

3 Pin and sew a segment from step 1 between two segments from step 2, rotating one of the step 2 segments. Press the seam allowances away from the center. Make 30 block centers.

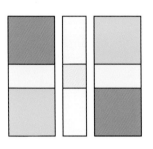 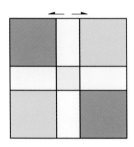

Make 30.

Piecing the A Blocks

1 Draw a diagonal line on the wrong side of each navy and lime-green 4" square. Place a marked square on a white 4" square with right sides together. Sew ¼" from the drawn line on each side, and then cut on the drawn line. Make 60 navy-and-white and 60 green-and-white half-square-triangle units. Press the seam allowances toward the darker fabrics and trim the units to 3½" square.

Make 60 of each.

Trimming Tip

When trimming the half-square-triangle units, use a square ruler with a 45° angle line. Place the 45° angle line over the seam line when trimming.

2 Sew a navy-and-white half-square-triangle unit, a white 2" x 3½" rectangle, and a green-and-white half-square-triangle unit together as shown. Press the seam allowances toward the white rectangle. Make 30 top/bottom row units.

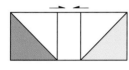

Make 30.

3 Repeat step 2, reversing the positions of the half-square-triangle units. Make 30 side units.

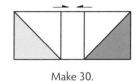

Make 30.

4 Lay out one block center, two top/bottom rows, two side units, and four white 3½" squares as shown. Pin and sew the pieces into three rows. Press the seam allowances as indicated by the arrows. Pin and sew the rows together. Press as shown. Make 15 of block A.

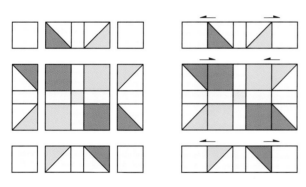

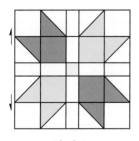

Block A.
Make 15.

Piecing the B Blocks

1 Sew a navy 3½" strip, a white 8" strip, and a lime-green 3½" strip together to make a strip set. Press the seam allowances toward the white strip. Make three strip sets. Cut 30 segments, 3½" wide.

Make 3 strip sets.
Cut 30 segments.

2 Lay out two segments from step 1, one block center, and two white 3½" x 8" rectangles as shown. Sew the center pieces into a row and press the seam allowances toward the white rectangles. Pin and sew the rows together. Press the seam allowances outward. Make 15 of block B.

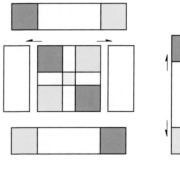

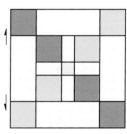

Block B.
Make 15.

Assembling the Quilt Top

1 Lay out the A and B blocks in six rows with five blocks per row, alternating the blocks as shown in the assembly diagram below.

2 Pin and sew the blocks into rows. Press the seam allowances in opposite directions from row to row.

3 Pin and sew the rows together, finishing the quilt top. Press the seam allowances open.

Finishing the Quilt

1 Cut the backing fabric in half to create two 90"-long pieces. Remove the selvages and sew the two halves together using a ½" seam allowance; press the seam allowances to one side. Trim the backing to approximately 80" x 90".

2 Layer the backing, batting, and quilt top. Baste the three layers together using your preferred method.

3 Quilt as desired. I echo quilted an allover design of paisleys, swirls, and curves.

4 Referring to "Binding a Quilt" on page 77, bind your quilt using the 2½"-wide strips.

Quilt assembly

"The North Star," designed and made by Melissa Corry.
Fabrics are Chromatics by the AGF In-House Studio for Art Gallery Fabrics.

When I look at this quilt, the white background seems to pop out, creating a twinkling, pixilated star—hence its name. The juxtaposition of large and small pieces yields an amazing sense of movement. This queen-size quilt is entirely strip pieced and quick to make. Choose two main fabrics and a background and you'll be done in no time.

Finished quilt:
91½" x 91½",
queen size

Finished block:
14" x 14"

Materials

Yardage is based on 42"-wide fabric.

4⅝ yards of white solid for block backgrounds

3¾ yards of gray print for blocks

2½ yards of yellow print for blocks and sashing*

⅞ yard of fabric for binding*

8½ yards of fabric for backing

101" x 101" piece of batting

If you wish to bind the quilt with the same yellow print used for blocks and sashing, as in the quilt shown, you'll need a total of 3¾ yards.

Cutting

From the yellow print, cut:
  5 strips, 5½" x 42"
  5 strips, 4½" x 42"
  3 strips, 3½" x 42"
  1 strip, 3½" x 12"
  3 strips, 2½" x 42"
  1 square, 5½" x 5½"
  1 strip, 1½" x 28"
  1 strip, 1½" x 14"

From the gray print, cut:
  5 strips, 5½" x 42"
  8 strips, 4½" x 42"
  1 strip, 4½" x 12"
  8 strips, 3½" x 42"
  8 strips, 2½" x 42"; from *3 of the strips* cut a
    total of:
    2 strips, 2½" x 28"
    1 strip, 2½" x 12"
    1 strip, 2½" x 14"
  1 rectangle, 4½" x 5½"

From the white solid, cut:
  3 strips, 9½" x 42"
  8 strips, 5½" x 42"
  1 strip, 5½" x 12"
  1 square, 5½" x 5½"
  5 strips, 2½" x 42"
  2 strips, 12½" x 42"
  18 strips, 1½" x 42"; crosscut into:
    18 strips, 1½" x 25½"
    6 strips, 1½" x 13½"

From the binding fabric, cut:
  10 strips, 2½" x 42"

Piecing the Blocks

1 Referring to "Strip Piecing" on page 74, sew a yellow 2½" x 42" strip, a gray 3½" x 42" strip, and a white 9½" x 42" strip together as shown. Press the seam allowances toward the yellow strip. Make three strip sets. Cut 36 segments, 2½" wide, for row 1.

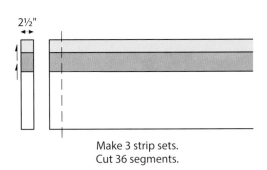

2½"

Make 3 strip sets.
Cut 36 segments.

2 Sew together a gray 2½" x 42" strip, a yellow 3½" x 42" strip, a gray 4½" x 42" strip, and a white 5½" x 42" strip to make a strip set. Press the seam allowances toward the white strip. Make three strip sets. Repeat with the 12"-long strips to make one strip set 12" long. Cut a total of 36 segments, 3½" wide, for row 2.

3½"

Make 3 strip sets 42" long and 1 strip set 12" long.
Cut 36 segments.

3 Sew together a white 2½" x 42" strip, a gray 3½" x 42" strip, a yellow 4½" x 42" strip, and a gray 5½" x 42" strip to make a strip set. Press the seam allowances toward the white strip. Make five strip sets. Cut 36 segments, 4½" wide, for row 3.

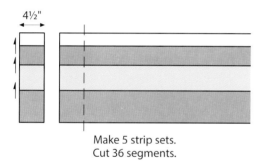

4½"

Make 5 strip sets.
Cut 36 segments.

4 Sew together a white 5½" x 42" strip, a gray 4½" x 42" strip, and a yellow 5½" x 42" strip to make a strip set. Press the seam allowances toward the yellow strip. Make five strip sets. Cut 35 segments, 5½" wide, for row 4.

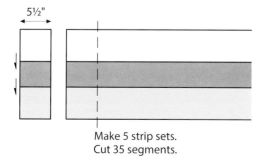

5½"

Make 5 strip sets.
Cut 35 segments.

The Details

What gives this quilt all its movement is that tiny little sashing that links the chains. And the strips *are* tiny. Take care when working with these small strips not to stretch the fabrics when piecing or pressing—they can be easily distorted because they're long and skinny. When you add them to your block layout, take time to align and pin the centers carefully. Having the 1" squares perfectly aligned will make your chains flow and not detract from the wonderful diagonal movement.

5 To make the final row, sew together the white 5½" square, the gray 4½" x 5½" rectangle, and the yellow 5½" square as shown. Press the seam allowances toward the yellow square.

Make 1.

6 Lay out the rows in order. Pin and sew them together. Press the seam allowances open. Make 36 blocks.

Row 1
Row 2
Row 3
Row 4

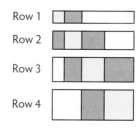

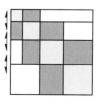

Make 36.

Piecing the Sashing

1 Sew a gray 2½" x 28" strip to each side of the yellow 1½" x 28" strip. Press the seam allowances toward the gray strips. Cut 17 segments, 1½" wide.

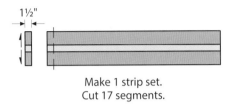

Make 1 strip set.
Cut 17 segments.

2 Sew the gray 2½" x 14" strip and the yellow 1½" x 14" strip together. Press the seam allowances toward the gray strip. Cut eight segments, 1½" wide.

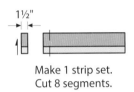

Make 1 strip set.
Cut 8 segments.

3 Sew a gray 2½" x 42" strip and a white 12½" x 42" strip together. Press the seam allowances toward the gray strip. Make two strip sets. Cut 42 segments, 1½" wide.

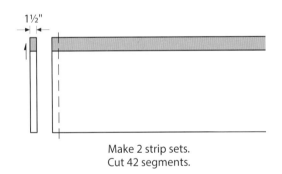

Make 2 strip sets.
Cut 42 segments.

Assembling the Quilt Top

1 Lay out the blocks in six rows with six blocks per row, rotating the blocks as shown in the assembly diagram above right. Add the white 1½" x 25½" strips, white 1½" x 13½" strips, and sashing segments around the blocks to create the sashing.

2 Sew the sashing strips and sashing segments into rows. Press the seam allowances toward the sashing strips. Pin and sew the sashing segments and blocks into rows. Press the seam allowances toward the sashing.

3 Pin and sew the rows together, finishing the quilt top. Press the seam allowances open.

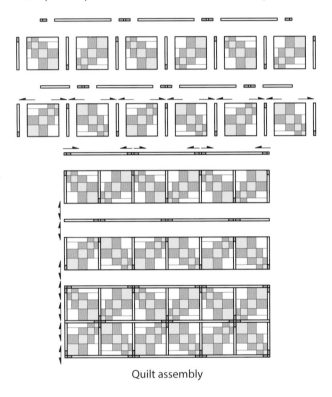

Quilt assembly

Finishing the Quilt

1 Cut the backing fabric into three 102"-long pieces. Remove the selvages and sew the three pieces together using a ½" seam allowance. Press the seam allowances to one side. Trim the backing to approximately 102" x 102".

2 Layer the backing, batting, and quilt top. Baste the three layers together using your preferred method.

3 Quilt as desired. I quilted an allover exploding-star design.

4 Referring to "Binding a Quilt" on page 77, bind your quilt using the 2½"-wide strips.

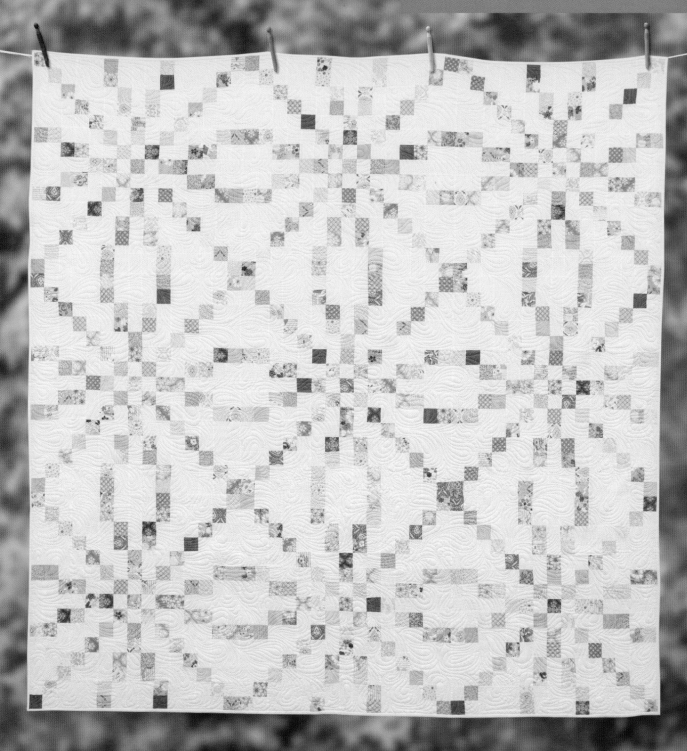

"An Irish Braid," designed and made by Melissa Corry.
Fabrics are Hello Luscious by Basic Grey for Moda.

I designed "An Irish Braid" well before I began working on this book, but I knew it deserved a place within these pages. I've always loved its intricately modern twist, and I hope it will become a long-time favorite of yours as it has been for me. This is the perfect project for working with 2½"-wide precut strips.

Finished quilt:
90½" x 90½", queen size

Finished block:
30" x 30"

Materials

Yardage is based on 42"-wide fabric.

6³⁄₈ yards of white solid for block backgrounds

3¼ yards *total* of assorted prints for blocks*

⁷⁄₈ yard of fabric for binding

8½ yards of fabric for backing

100" x 100" piece of batting

If using precuts, select 40 strips, 2½" x 42".

Add Variety

The assorted prints in this quilt are cut into 2½"-wide strips. Using a Jelly Roll or similar bundle of 2½"-wide strips is a great way to save cutting time and add lots of variety to your quilt. You only need 40 strips, so grab a precut packet and get started.

Cutting

From the assorted prints, cut:
   40 strips, 2½" x 42"; *crosscut 5* strips into
      81 squares, 2½" x 2½"

From the white solid, cut:
   62 strips, 2½" x 42"; *crosscut 27* strips into:
      144 rectangles, 2½" x 4½"
      36 rectangles, 2½" x 8½"
   12 strips, 4½" x 42"; crosscut into 72
      rectangles, 4½" x 6½"

From the binding fabric, cut:
   10 strips, 2½" x 42"

Piecing the Strip Units

1 Referring to "Strip Piecing" on page 74, sew a print and a white 2½" x 42" strip together as shown. Press the seam allowances open. Make 35 strip sets. Cut 540 segments, 2½" wide.

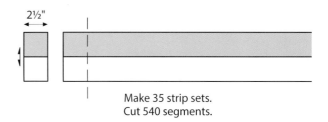

Make 35 strip sets.
Cut 540 segments.

2 Pin and sew two segments together to make a four-patch unit. Press the seam allowances open. Make 108 units.

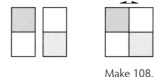

Make 108.

3 Pin and sew two segments from step 1 together with print squares adjoining. Press the seam allowances open. Make 144 one-sided four-patch units.

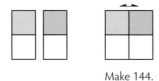

Make 144.

Piecing the A Blocks

1 Sew a four-patch unit and a white 4½" x 6½" rectangle together as shown. Press the seam allowances toward the rectangle. Make 72 side units.

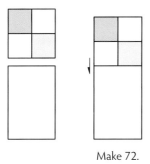

Make 72.

2 Pin and sew together a print 2½" square between two white 2½" x 4½" rectangles. Press the seam allowances toward the rectangles. Make 36 center units.

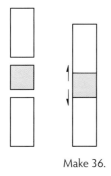

Make 36.

3 Pin and sew together two side units and one center unit as shown. Press the seam allowances open. Make 36 of block A.

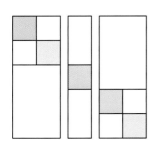 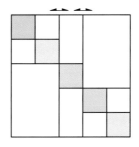

Block A.
Make 36.

The Details

Strip piecing really speeds up the construction of this quilt, but remember, you want accuracy as well as speed. There are a lot of seams to align in this quilt. Here are a few tips that will help.

- Shorten the stitch length when sewing strip sets to keep cut stitches from coming undone.
- When pressing strip-pieced fabrics, take care to gently press the seam allowances open. It's very easy to stretch these long strips of fabric, especially when you've been pressing for a while and aren't paying attention.
- When you're ready to subcut the strip sets, you may be tempted to stack them to save time. But rather than stack them, spread them apart on your cutting mat. (See "Strip Piecing," step 4, on page 74.) This way you can cut multiple strip sets at once, but you won't have any slipping where stacked seam allowances don't want to lie flat.

Piecing the B Blocks

1 Pin and sew together two one-sided four-patch units and a white 2½" x 4½" rectangle as shown. Press the seam allowances open. Make 36 left-side units.

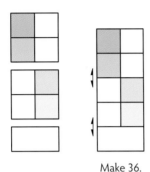

Make 36.

2 Pin and sew together two one-sided four-patch units and a white 2½" x 4½" rectangle as shown. Press the seam allowances open. Make 36 right-side units.

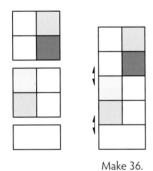

Make 36.

3 Sew a print 2½" square to a white 2½" x 8½" rectangle. Press the seam allowances open. Make 36 center units.

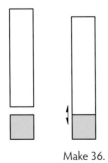

Make 36.

4 Pin and sew together a left-side unit, a center unit, and a right-side unit as shown. Press the seam allowances open. Make 36 of block B.

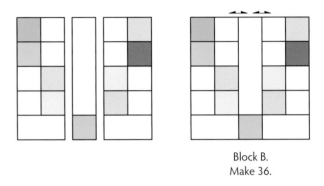

Block B.
Make 36.

Piecing the C Blocks

1 Pin and sew together two four-patch units and one strip-set segment so the print squares alternate. Press the seam allowances open. Make 18 side units.

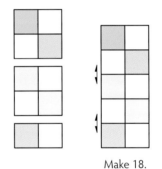

Make 18.

2 Sew together two strip-set segments and one print 2½" square so the print and white squares alternate. Press the seam allowances open. Make nine center units.

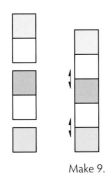

Make 9.

3 Pin and sew together two side units and one center unit as shown. Press the seam allowances open. Make nine of block C.

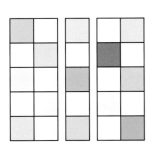 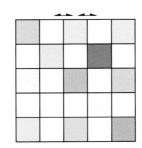

Block C.
Make 9.

Piecing the ABC Blocks

Lay out four A blocks, four B blocks, and one C block in three vertical rows. Pin and sew the blocks into rows. Press the seam allowances open. Pin and sew the rows together. Press the seam allowances open. Make nine of block ABC.

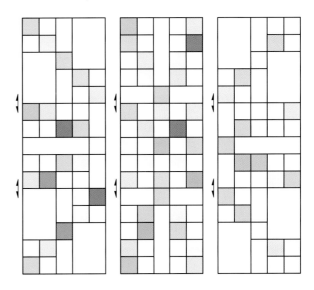

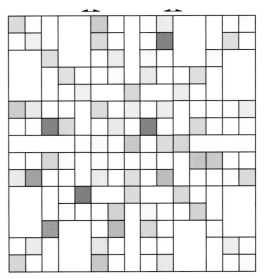

Block ABC.
Make 9.

Assembling the Quilt Top

1 Lay out the ABC blocks in three rows with three blocks per row as shown in the assembly diagram below.

2 Pin and sew the blocks into rows. Press the seam allowances open. Pin and sew the rows together, finishing the quilt top. Press the seam allowances open.

Finishing the Quilt

1 Cut the backing fabric into three 102"-long pieces. Remove the selvages and sew the three pieces together using a ½" seam allowance; press the seam allowances to one side. Trim the backing to approximately 102" x 102".

2 Layer the backing, batting, and quilt top. Baste the three layers together using your preferred method.

3 Quilt as desired. I echo quilted an allover paisley design.

4 Referring to "Binding a Quilt" on page 77, bind your quilt using the 2½"-wide strips.

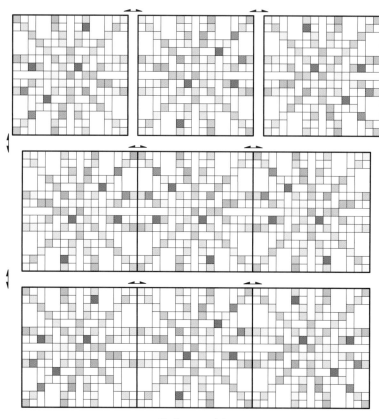

Quilt assembly

Modern Patchwork

Modern quilting is becoming vastly popular in the quilting world. It's a design concept that has been defined and redefined, and each of its participants would probably explain it differently. The characteristics often found in modern quilting include using bold colors, embracing minimalism, incorporating asymmetry of design, and employing expansive amounts of negative space. I see modern design as a way for individuals to express their personal creativity with no boundaries. It is a wonderful way to push the limits of your own design concepts.

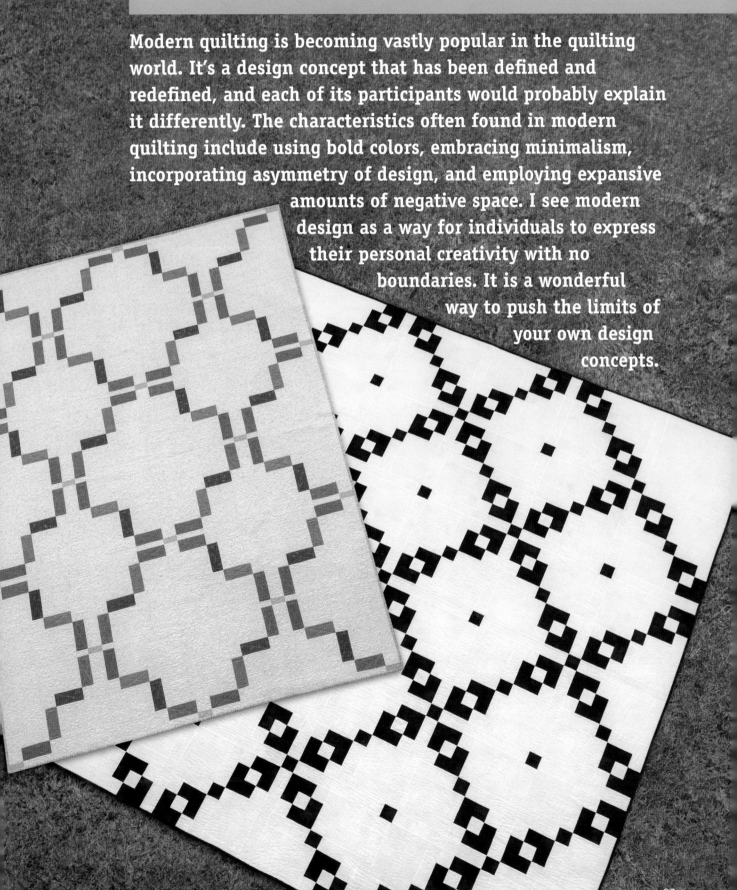

Unraveled

Using the asymmetrical approach of modern quilting turns this simple chain into a whole new design concept. It's as if the chain has truly unraveled. The design possibilities are endless, so have some fun with this one and make it your own.

Finished quilt:
63½" x 75½",
lap size

Finished block:
9" x 9"

Materials

Yardage is based on 42"-wide fabric.

4 yards of white solid for blocks

1 yard *total* of assorted prints for blocks

²/₃ yard of fabric for binding

4⅞ yards of fabric for backing

73" x 85" piece of batting

Add Variety

This quilt is perfect for using up some of those stacks of precuts or cleaning out your scrap drawers. Both are great options to bring lots of color and variety to your quilt.

Cutting

From the assorted prints, cut:
89 squares, 3½" x 3½"

From the white solid, cut:
7 squares, 9½" x 9½"
32 strips, 3½" x 42"; crosscut into:
71 rectangles, 3½" x 9½"
46 rectangles, 3½" x 6½"
68 squares, 3½" x 3½"

From the binding fabric, cut:
8 strips, 2½" x 42"

Piecing the Blocks

1 Sew a print 3½" square to a white 3½" x 6½" rectangle. Press the seam allowances toward the print square. Make 46 units.

Make 46.

2 Sew a print 3½" square between two white 3½" squares. Press the seam allowances toward the print square. Make 23 units.

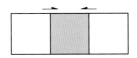

Make 23.

3 Pin and sew two units from step 1 and one unit from step 2 together as shown. Press the seam allowances away from the center. Make 23 blocks.

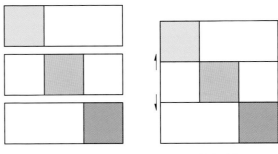

Make 23.

The Details

Because of the asymmetrical design of this quilt, balancing the colors in the layout is crucial. Once you have an arrangement you like, snap a quick picture of the blocks and then view it on your computer, tablet, or phone. It's a great way to easily see if your colors are balanced and where you might want to do a little rearranging.

Assembling the Quilt Top

1 Lay out the blocks and white 9½" squares in six rows with five blocks per row, rotating the pieced blocks as shown in the assembly diagram above right. Add the white 3½" x 9½" rectangles and print and white 3½" squares around the blocks to create the sashing.

2 Sew the sashing rectangles and squares into rows. Press the seam allowances toward the sashing rectangles. Pin and sew the sashing rectangles, pieced blocks, and squares into rows. Press the seam allowances toward the sashing rectangles.

3 Pin and sew the rows together, finishing the quilt top. Press the seam allowances open.

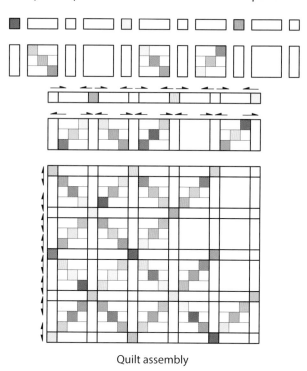

Quilt assembly

Finishing the Quilt

1 Cut the backing fabric in half to create two 87"-long pieces. Remove the selvages and sew the two halves together using a ½" seam allowance. Press the seam allowances to one side. Trim the backing to approximately 74" x 86".

2 Layer the backing, batting, and quilt top. Baste the three layers together using your preferred method.

3 Quilt as desired. I quilted straight lines through all the print squares and added small, medium, and large swirls throughout the quilt background.

4 Referring to "Binding a Quilt" on page 77, bind your quilt using the 2½"-wide strips.

"Pick Up Sticks," designed and made by Melissa Corry.
Fabrics are Botanics by Carolyn Friedlander for Robert Kaufman Fabrics.

Did you play with pick-up sticks as a child? During childhood visits to my grandmother's house, my siblings and I enjoyed many fun-filled hours with that game. The classic pastime inspired this simple geometric design, which allows you to highlight favorite bold prints or solids for a perfect splash of color. This would make a wonderful quilt for a child's bedroom or an ideal quilt for a college dorm room.

**Finished quilt:
69" x 91½",
twin size**

**Finished block:
14" x 14"**

Materials

Yardage is based on 42"-wide fabric.

6⅜ yards of white print for block backgrounds

⅜ yard *each* of orange, teal, gold, and gray prints or solids for blocks

⅛ yard of light-blue print for sashing cornerstones

¾ yard of fabric for binding

5⅔ yards of fabric for backing

79" x 101" piece of batting

Cutting

From *each* of the orange and gold prints, cut:
2 strips, 5½" x 42"

From the white print, cut:
4 strips, 12½" x 42"
2 strips, 9½" x 42"
6 strips, 7½" x 42"
4 strips, 5½" x 42"
2 strips, 2½" x 42"
4 strips, 14½" x 42"; crosscut into:
   30 rectangles, 3" x 14½"
   28 rectangles, 1½" x 14½"
2 strips, 1½" x 42"; crosscut into 17 rectangles,
   1½" x 3"

From *each* of the teal and gray prints, cut:
4 strips, 2½" x 42"

From the light-blue print, cut:
2 strips, 1½" x 42"; crosscut into 18 rectangles,
   1½" x 3"

From the binding fabric, cut:
9 strips, 2½" x 42"

Piecing the Blocks

1 Referring to "Strip Piecing" on page 74, sew an orange 5½" x 42" strip and a white 9½" x 42" strip together as shown. Press the seam allowances toward the orange strip. Make two strip sets. Cut 24 segments, 2½" wide, for row 1.

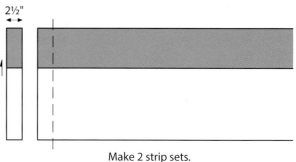

2½"

Make 2 strip sets.
Cut 24 segments.

2 Sew together a white 5½" x 42" strip, a teal 2½" x 42" strip, and a white 7½" x 42" strip to make a strip set. Press the seam allowances toward the teal strip. Make four strip sets. Cut 24 segments, 5½" wide, for row 2.

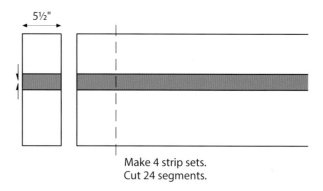

5½"

Make 4 strip sets.
Cut 24 segments.

3 Sew together a white 7½" x 42" strip, a gold 5½" x 42" strip, and a white 2½" x 42" strip to make a strip set. Press the seam allowances toward the gold strip. Make two strip sets. Cut 24 segments, 2½" wide, for row 3.

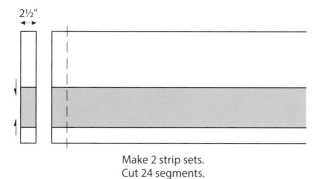

2½"

Make 2 strip sets.
Cut 24 segments.

4 Sew together a white 12½" x 42" strip and a gray 2½" x 42" strip. Press the seam allowances toward the gray strip. Make four strip sets. Cut 24 segments, 5½" wide, for row 4.

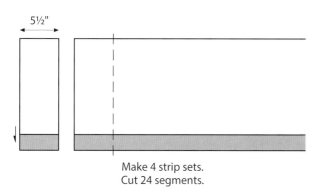

5½"

Make 4 strip sets.
Cut 24 segments.

5 Lay out the rows as shown. Pin and sew the rows together. Press the seam allowances open. Make 24 blocks.

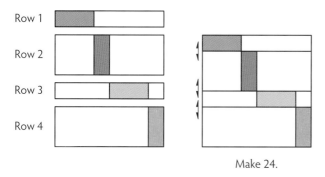

Row 1

Row 2

Row 3

Row 4

Make 24.

The Details

This quilt highlights lots and lots of negative space in the background. You can fill that space with whatever fabric that you like. You can use a solid—and it doesn't have to be white—or a light print, as I did. If you choose a print, I suggest that you select one that's nondirectional; it would be extremely difficult to keep the print going in one direction because of the strip piecing. A small-scale, subtle print will give you the most stress-free piecing and a wonderful outcome.

Assembling the Quilt Top

1 Lay out the blocks in six rows with four blocks per row, rotating the blocks as shown in the assembly diagram below. Add the white 3" x 14½" rectangles vertically between the blocks and the white 1½" x 14½" rectangles horizontally between the blocks to create the sashing. Place the white and light-blue 1½" x 3" rectangles in alternating positions within the horizontal sashing rows to complete the chain design.

2 Sew the horizontal sashing and cornerstone rectangles into rows. Press the seam allowances toward the sashing. Pin and sew the vertical sashing rectangles and the blocks into rows. Press the seam allowances toward the sashing.

3 Pin and sew the rows together, finishing the quilt top. Press the seam allowances open.

Finishing the Quilt

1 Cut the backing fabric in half to create two 101"-long pieces. Remove the selvages and sew the two halves together using a ½" seam allowance; press the seam allowances to one side. Trim the backing to approximately 79" x 101".

2 Layer the backing, batting, and quilt top. Baste the three layers together using your preferred method.

3 Quilt as desired. I quilted framed Xs in the chain rectangles and meandering tiles throughout the background.

4 Referring to "Binding a Quilt" on page 77, bind your quilt using the 2½"-wide strips.

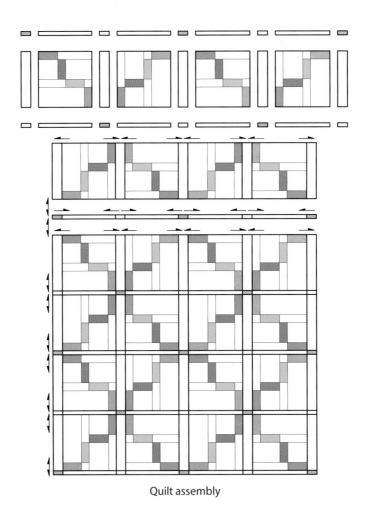

Quilt assembly

Coins in the Fountain

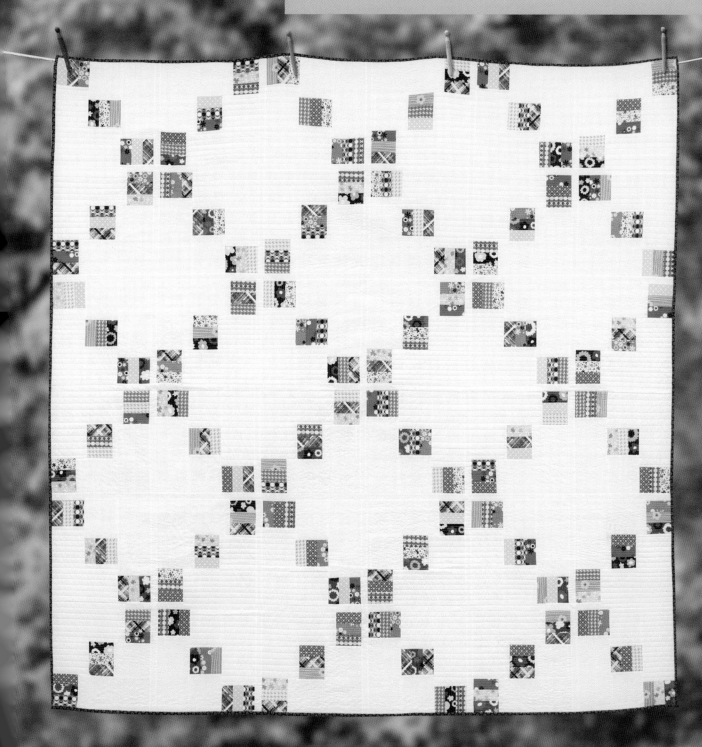

"Coins in the Fountain," designed and made by Melissa Corry.
Fabrics are Nördika by Jeni Baker for Art Gallery Fabrics.

Coin quilts are great fun to make, and I definitely wanted to include one in an Irish Chain interpretation. After playing around with several design ideas, I knew this was it. The small groupings of pieced coins create the illusion of a circular space in the background that reminds me of tossing coins in a fountain. Make a wish!

Finished quilt:
86½" x 86½",
full size

Finished block:
13½" x 13½"

Materials

Yardage is based on 42"-wide fabric.

6 yards of white solid for block backgrounds and sashing

2 yards *total* of assorted prints for blocks

¾ yard of fabric for binding

8¼ yards of fabric for backing

96" x 96" piece of batting

Add Variety

With lots of little rectangles, this project is your perfect opportunity to clean out that scrap drawer, basket, or bin while adding variety, color, and interest to your quilt.

Cutting

From the assorted prints, cut:
324 rectangles, 2" x 4"

From the white solid, cut:
32 strips*, 5" x 42"; crosscut into:
72 rectangles, 5" x 10½"
72 rectangles, 5" x 5½"
26 strips**, 1½" x 42"; crosscut *15 strips* into
30 rectangles, 1½" x 14"

From the binding fabric, cut:
9 strips, 2½" x 42"

If your fabric has at least 42" of usable width, 29 strips will be enough.

**If your fabric has at least 42" of usable width, 21 strips will be enough.*

Piecing the Blocks

1 Choose three 2" x 4" rectangles of assorted prints and sew them together as shown. Press the seam allowances in one direction. Make 108 coin units.

Make 108.

Keep It Casual

Don't stress about the color placement in your coin units. Just keep the layout fun and random. You will have plenty of opportunity to shuffle them around later for a balanced look.

2 Sew a coin unit to a white 5" x 10½" rectangle. Press the seam allowances toward the white rectangle. Make 72 side units.

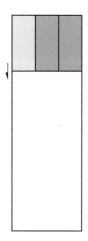

Make 72.

3 Sew a coin unit between two white 5" x 5½" rectangles. Press the seam allowances toward the white rectangles. Make 36 center units.

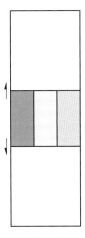

Make 36.

4 Sew two side units and one center unit together as shown. Press the seam allowances open. Make 36 blocks.

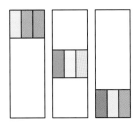 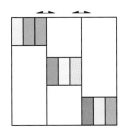

Make 36.

Assembling the Quilt Top

1 Lay out the blocks in six rows with six blocks per row, rotating the blocks as shown in the assembly diagram on page 38. Place the white 1½" x 14" rectangles between the blocks as shown to create the vertical sashing.

The Details

This quilt is quilted entirely with straight lines. When quilting straight lines, it's important to have the right tools. If you're quilting on a domestic machine, a walking foot will save you a million headaches. The feed dogs on the top of the foot will work with the feed dogs on your machine to evenly move the fabric through your machine, avoiding bubbles or pleats in the back of your quilt. If you're using a long-arm machine, you'll need a straight quilting ruler. It's extremely difficult to make straight lines on a long-arm machine without one.

2 Sew the 11 white 1½" x 42" strips together end to end. Press the seam allowances to one side. Cut into five strips, 86½" long, to make the horizontal sashing. Place the sashing strips in the layout between the block rows.

Balancing the Layout

Now's the time to arrange and rearrange the colored coin units. Spend some time playing with the placement of your blocks until the layout is balanced and pleasing to your eye.

3 Pin and sew the sashing rectangles and blocks into rows. Press the seam allowances toward the sashing rectangles. Pin and sew the rows and sashing strips together, finishing the quilt top. Press the seam allowances toward the sashing strips.

Finishing the Quilt

1 Cut the backing fabric into three 99"-long pieces. Remove the selvages and sew the three pieces together using a ½" seam allowance; press the seam allowances to one side. Trim the backing to approximately 98" x 98".

2 Layer the backing, batting, and quilt top. Baste the three layers together using your preferred method.

3 Quilt as desired. I first quilted straight lines ¼" apart on all the coins, and then stitched straight lines ¾" apart throughout the background, reversing the direction of the lines in each background section.

4 Referring to "Binding a Quilt" on page 77, bind your quilt using the 2½"-wide strips.

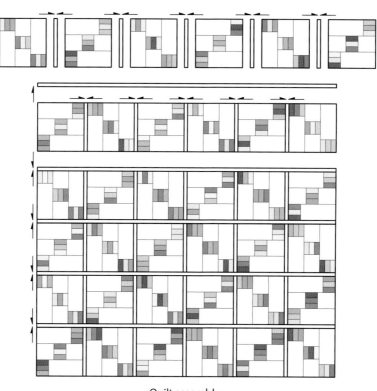

Quilt assembly

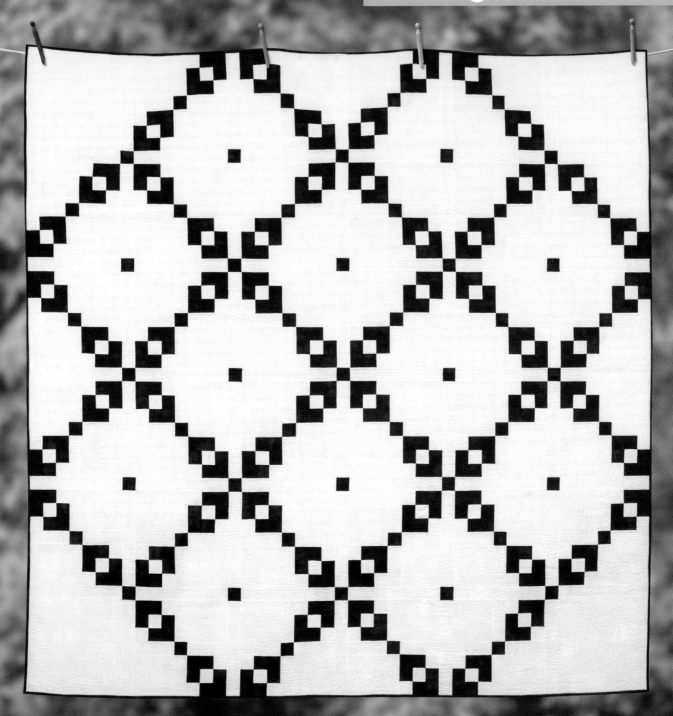

"String of Pearls," designed and made by Melissa Corry.
Fabrics are Grunge Basics by Basic Grey for Moda.

Bold, simple quilt designs are always a joy to make and always classy— just like a string of pearls. The lines of this quilt are sharp and clean, made even more so with fabrics of basic, sophisticated black and white. And with the dark fabric of the chain omitted from the corners of the blocks, you can see several strings of pearls, all connected.

Finished quilt:
94½" x 94½", queen size

Finished block:
14" x 14"

Materials

Yardage is based on 42"-wide fabric.

7¼ yards of white textured solid for block backgrounds and sashing

2 yards of black textured solid for blocks and sashing squares

⅞ yard of fabric for binding

9 yards of fabric for backing

104" x 104" piece of batting

Cutting

From the black solid, cut:

8 strips, 4½" x 42"

12 strips, 2½" x 42"; crosscut *2 strips* into 25 squares, 2½" x 2½"

From the white solid, cut:

4 squares, 14½" x 14½"

4 strips, 6½" x 42"

11 strips, 8½" x 42"; crosscut into 64 rectangles, 6½" x 8½"

12 strips, 2½" x 42"

4 strips, 14½" x 42"; crosscut into 60 rectangles, 2½" x 14½"

From the binding fabric, cut:

10 strips, 2½" x 42"

Piecing the Blocks

1 Referring to "Strip Piecing" on page 74, sew a black 4½" x 42" strip to a white 2½" x 42" white strip. Press the seam allowances toward the black strip. Make eight strip sets. Cut 128 segments, 2½" wide.

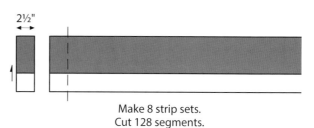

Make 8 strip sets.
Cut 128 segments.

2 Sew a black 2½" x 42" strip to each side of a white 2½" x 42" strip to make a strip set. Press the seam allowances toward the black strips. Make four strip sets. Cut 64 segments, 2½" wide.

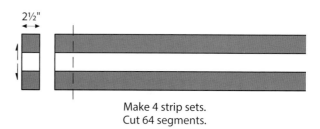

Make 4 strip sets.
Cut 64 segments.

3 Pin and sew two segments from step 1 and one segment from step 2 together as shown. Press the seam allowances open. Make 64 corner units.

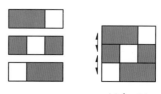

Make 64.

4 Sew a corner unit and a white 6½" x 8½" rectangle together. Press the seam allowances toward the white rectangle. Make 64 top/bottom rows.

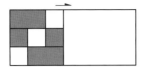

Make 64.

5 Sew a white 6½" x 42" strip to each side of a black 2½" x 42" strip. Press the seam allowances toward the white strips. Make two strip sets. Cut 32 segments, 2½" wide, for the block center rows.

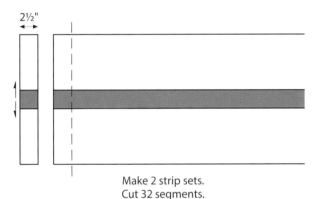

Make 2 strip sets.
Cut 32 segments.

6 Pin and sew two top/bottom rows and one center row together. Press the seam allowances toward the center row. Make 32 blocks.

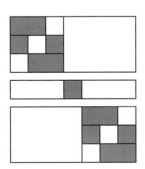

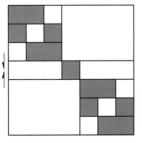

Make 32.

The Details

The simple black and white textured solids in this quilt add to the simplistic design, creating a classic look. Keeping your version as a two-color quilt will retain the stylish statement. If you want to use a print, choose a tonal fabric—something that reads as a solid—so it looks like one color throughout the quilt. And to really make your chain pop, it's worth the extra effort to quilt with white thread on white and dark thread on dark.

Assembling the Quilt Top

1 Lay out the blocks and white 14½" squares in six rows with six blocks per row, rotating the pieced blocks as shown in the assembly diagram below. Add white 2½" x 14½" rectangles and black 2½" squares between the blocks to create the sashing and corner squares.

2 Sew the sashing rectangles and corner squares into rows. Press the seam allowances toward the sashing rectangles. Pin and sew the sashing rectangles and blocks into rows. Press the seam allowances toward the sashing rectangles.

3 Pin and sew the rows together, finishing the quilt top. Press the seam allowances open.

Finishing the Quilt

1 Cut the backing fabric into three 108"-long pieces. Remove the selvages and sew the three pieces together using a ½" seam allowance; press the seam allowances to one side. Trim the backing to approximately 108" x 108".

2 Layer the backing, batting, and quilt top. Baste the three layers together using your preferred method.

3 Quilt as desired. I quilted wavy lines in the background and large pebbles throughout the chains.

4 Referring to "Binding a Quilt" on page 77, bind your quilt using the 2½"-wide strips.

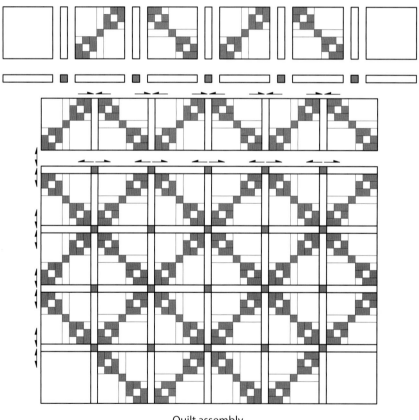

Quilt assembly

Improvisational Piecing

Improvisational piecing is a terrifically fun way to make a quilt because there really are no rules. The traditional accuracy of quilting loses some of its importance in improvisational design, since most of your fabrics are going to be stacked, slashed, or trimmed. This makes for carefree piecing, which has the added bonus of being fast! I think you'll find improvisational piecing to be very freeing.

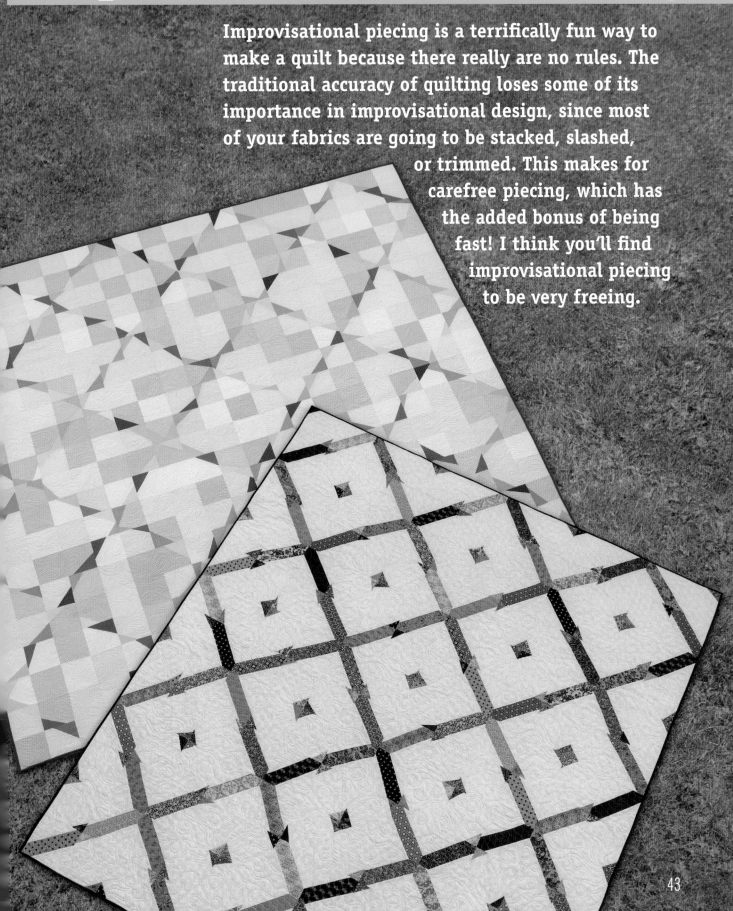

Charm Bracelet

"Charm Bracelet," designed and made by Melissa Corry.
Fabrics are True Colors by Heather Bailey for Free Spirit Fabrics.

This adorable, whimsical quilt goes together quickly, making it the perfect go-to baby blanket when you're in a pinch for a gift. And because of the improvisational nature, no two quilts will ever turn out the same. It's a favorite that I'm sure I'll make over and over again.

Finished quilt: 42" x 42", baby size

Finished block: 8" x 8"

Materials

Yardage is based on 42"-wide fabric.

1½ yards of white solid for block backgrounds and sashing

1 yard *total* of assorted prints for blocks and sashing squares

½ yard of fabric for binding

2¼ yards of fabric for backing

50" x 50" piece of batting

Add Variety

Here's another quilt that's ideal for using one of those favorite fabric lines you've been saving. Or, go through your scrap bins and pull out some treasured bits and pieces.

Cutting

From the assorted prints, cut:

80 squares, 3½" x 3½"

25 squares, 2½" x 2½"

From the white solid, cut:

6 strips, 3½" x 42"; crosscut into 64 squares, 3½" x 3½"

10 strips, 2½" x 42"; crosscut into 40 rectangles, 2½" x 8½"

From the binding fabric, cut:

5 strips, 2½" x 42"

Piecing the Blocks

1 Sew two different 3½" print squares and one white 3½" square together in a row. Press the seam allowances toward the print squares. Make 32 top/bottom rows.

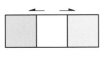

Make 32.

2 Sew white 3½" squares to opposite sides of a print 3½" square. Press the seam allowances toward the print square. Make 16 center rows.

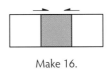

Make 16.

3 Sew two top/bottom rows and one center row together. Press the seam allowances away from the center. Make 16 Nine Patch blocks.

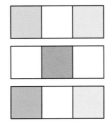

Make 16.

4 Referring to "Trimming Blocks at an Angle" on page 75, trim the Nine Patch blocks to 8½" x 8½".

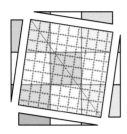 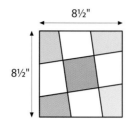

The Details

Take time to arrange and rearrange your blocks until you are pleased with the results. You'll be balancing colors as well as shapes and sizes. The sashing corner squares can be a big help in this regard, so arrange your blocks first and then add the corner squares.

Assembling the Quilt Top

1 Lay out the blocks in four rows with four blocks per row, rotating the blocks as shown in the assembly diagram above right or as desired. Add the white 2½" x 8½" rectangles and print 2½" squares around the blocks to create the sashing.

2 Sew the sashing rectangles and corner squares into rows. Press the seam allowances toward the sashing rectangles. Pin and sew the sashing rectangles and blocks into rows. Press the seam allowances toward the sashing rectangles.

3 Pin and sew the rows together, finishing the quilt top. Press the seam allowances open.

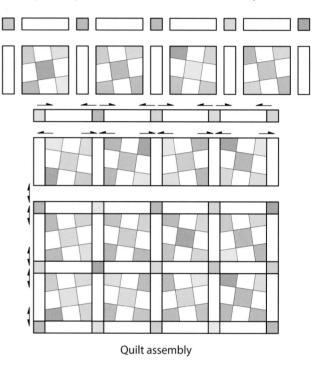

Quilt assembly

Finishing the Quilt

1 Cut the backing fabric into a 53"-long piece and a 27"-long piece. Remove the selvages. Cut the 27" piece into two pieces, 27" x 21"; sew the pieces together along the 21" width using a ½" seam allowance. Press the seam allowances to one side. Sew this to the 53"-long piece along the 53" length, using a ½" seam allowance. Press the seam allowances to one side. Trim the backing to approximately 53" x 53".

2 Layer the backing, batting, and quilt top. Baste the three layers together using your preferred method.

3 Quilt as desired. I used a meandering design throughout the background and echo quilted boxes in the print squares.

4 Referring to "Binding a Quilt" on page 77, bind your quilt using the 2½"-wide strips.

"Fractured," designed and made by Melissa Corry.
Fabrics are Little Black Dress 2 by Basic Grey for Moda.

This striking design uses free-form piecing and a mixed bag of angles to create a chain with fractured points. Wonderful black-and-cream prints work together in a monochromatic color scheme, softening the look and taking the edge off the jagged angles just a bit.

Finished quilt:
72½" x 84½",
twin size

Finished block:
12" x 12"

Materials

Yardage is based on 42"-wide fabric.

5⅜ yards of cream tone on tone for block backgrounds

2⅓ yards *total* of assorted medium to dark prints for blocks

¾ yard of fabric for binding

5¼ yards of fabric for backing

82" x 94" piece of batting

Cutting

From the assorted prints, cut:

84 squares, 3¼" x 3¼"; cut the squares in half diagonally to yield 168 triangles

84 rectangles, 2½" x 10"

From the cream tone on tone, cut:

14 strips, 6½" x 42"; crosscut into 84 squares, 6½" x 6½"

14 strips, 6" x 42"; crosscut into 84 squares, 6" x 6". Cut the squares in half diagonally to yield 168 triangles.

From the binding fabric, cut:

9 strips, 2½" x 42"

Piecing the A Blocks

1 Place two print triangles on opposite corners of a cream 6½" square with right sides together. Vary the position of the triangles to create points with random angles. Sew ¼" from the long edge of each triangle, and then trim along the triangle edges. Press the seam allowances toward the print triangles.

Varying Angles

The more you adjust the angles, the more "fractured" your quilt will look. Before you sew, hold a finger along the edge of the triangle and flip it back to ensure that it will extend past the edge of the background square. You'll quickly get the hang of how far you can vary the angles, but you can always do this little test first to double-check.

2 Align a 6½" square ruler with the unsewn corners of the cream square and trim the unit to 6½" x 6½" square to make block A. Make 84 blocks.

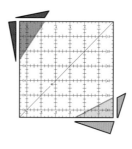 

Block A.
Make 84.

Piecing the B Blocks

1 Center a cream triangle on a print 2½" x 10" rectangle with right sides together as shown. Sew ¼" from the long edge of the triangle. Press the seam allowances toward the triangle. Repeat with a second cream triangle on the other side of the print rectangle, aligning the points of the triangles.

Align.

Centering the Triangles

When centering the cream triangles on the print rectangles, you don't need to measure the perfect center. You'll be trimming the block down to size, so you can simply eyeball it.

2 Referring to "Trimming Blocks at an Angle" on page 75, trim the unit to 6½" x 6½" to make block B. Make 84 blocks.

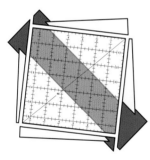 

Block B.
Make 84.

The Details

When trimming the lattice blocks (block B) in this quilt, don't be afraid to really play up the angles. The point is to avoid centering each block when trimming. The more you angle the ruler to one seam or another, the more angles you'll get in your chain. Just be sure that the edge of your trimming is indeed on the medium to dark lattice piece and not the background, otherwise you'll lose your chain altogether.

Piecing the AB Blocks

Lay out two A blocks and two B blocks as shown. Sew the blocks into two rows. Press the seam allowances open. Pin and sew the rows together. Press the seam allowances open. Make 42 of block AB.

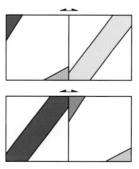 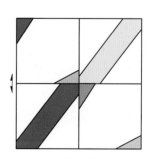

Make 42.

Assembling the Quilt Top

1 Lay out the AB blocks in seven rows with six blocks per row, rotating the blocks as shown in the assembly diagram below.

2 Pin and sew the blocks into rows. Press the seam allowances in opposite directions from row to row.

3 Pin and sew the rows together, finishing the quilt top. Press the seam allowances open.

Finishing the Quilt

1 Cut the backing fabric in half to create two 94"-long pieces. Remove the selvages and sew the two halves together along the long edges using a ½" seam allowance; press the seam allowances to one side. Trim the backing to approximately 83" x 94".

2 Layer the backing, batting, and quilt top. Baste the three layers together using your preferred method.

3 Quilt as desired. I quilted figure eights in the print rectangles and ribbons in the cream background.

4 Referring to "Binding a Quilt" on page 77, bind your quilt using the 2½"-wide strips.

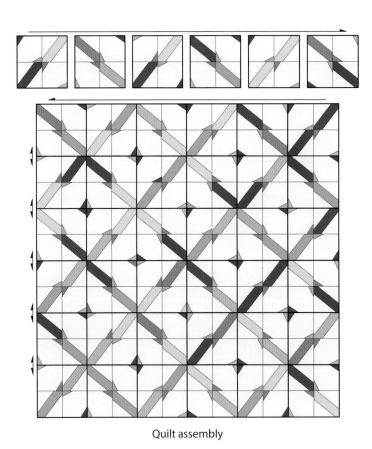

Quilt assembly

"End of the Rainbow," designed and made by Melissa Corry.
Fabrics are special scraps from her stash.

For a special "memory quilt," pull together scraps that are filled with personal significance. In this quilt are scraps from my very first quilt, each of my published quilts, each of my pattern quilts, and so on. Every time I look at it, I think of a different project I have made. It truly is the quilt I would want to find at the "end of the rainbow."

Finished quilt: 75½" x 75½", picnic size

Finished block: 12½" x 12½"

Materials

Yardage is based on 42"-wide fabric.

4 yards *total* of assorted light prints for block backgrounds

1 yard *total* of assorted red prints for blocks

1 yard *total* of assorted yellow prints for blocks

1 yard *total* of assorted orange prints for blocks

1 yard *total* of assorted green prints for blocks

1 yard *total* of assorted blue prints for blocks

1 yard *total* of assorted purple prints for blocks

⅔ yard of fabric for binding*

4¾ yards of fabric for backing**

85" x 85" piece of batting

See "The Details" on page 53 if you'd like to make a scrappy binding.

**If your fabric is less than 42" wide, you may need extra yardage to make your backing wide enough.*

Cutting

From the assorted light prints, cut:

72 rectangles, 3" x 9½"

72 rectangles, 3" x 6½"

72 rectangles, 3" x 4"

72 rectangles, 2½" x 3"

From the binding fabric, cut:

8 strips, 2½" x 42"

Piecing the Crazy-Patch Squares

1 Referring to "Crazy-Patch Piecing" on page 74, sew a 9" x 9" crazy-patch square. Make six squares from each of the six colors of prints, for a total of 36.

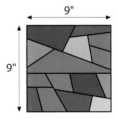

Make 6 of each color.

2 Cut each crazy-patch square into one 3" x 6" rectangle, two 3" x 5" rectangles, and two 3" x 4" rectangles as shown. You'll have a 3" square left over.

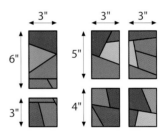

Piecing the Blocks

1 Sew one crazy-patch 3" x 4" rectangle and a light 3" x 9½" rectangle together as shown. Press the seam allowances toward the light rectangle. Make 12 of these rows from each color for a total of 72.

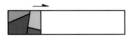

Make 12 of each color.

2 Sew a light 2½" x 3" rectangle, a crazy-patch 3" x 5" rectangle, and a light 3" x 6½" rectangle together as shown. Press the seam allowances toward the light rectangles. Make 12 of these rows from each color for a total of 72.

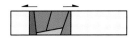

Make 12 of each color.

3 Sew a light 3" x 4" rectangle to each end of a crazy-patch 3" x 6" rectangle. Press the seam allowances toward the light rectangles. Make six of these rows from each color for a total of 36 rows.

Make 6 of each color.

4 Using rows of the same color, lay out two rows from step 1, two rows from step 2, and one row from step 3 as shown. Sew the rows together. Press the seam allowances open. Make six blocks of each color for a total of 36.

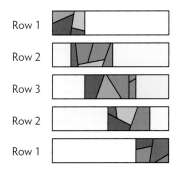

Row 1
Row 2
Row 3
Row 2
Row 1

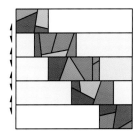

Make 6 of each color.

The Details

In keeping with the "scrapilicious" theme of this quilt, I added a scrappy binding for a really fun finish. First I measured the colored sections and added 3" for joining strips. (Add 4" if the binding will go around a corner.) I sewed the strips together in color order using a diagonal seam, and then I applied the binding to the quilt. For additional details, see the tutorials about scrappy bindings and custom bindings on my blog, www.happyquiltingmelissa.com.

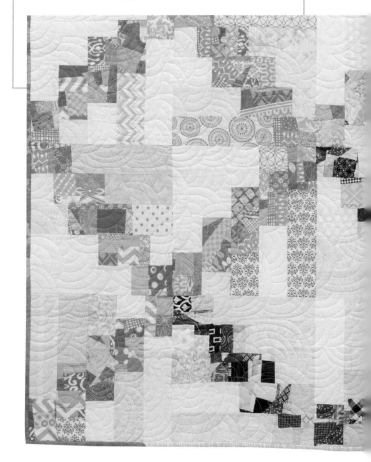

Assembling the Quilt Top

1 Lay out the blocks in six rows with six blocks per row, positioning the colors and alternating the blocks as shown in the assembly diagram below to form the chains as well as diagonal bands of rainbow colors.

2 Pin and sew the blocks into rows. Press the seam allowances in opposite directions from row to row.

3 Pin and sew the rows together, finishing the quilt top. Press the seam allowances open.

Finishing the Quilt

1 Cut the backing fabric in half to create two 85"-long pieces. Remove the selvages and sew the two halves together using a ½" seam allowance; press the seam allowances to one side to make a backing approximately 85" square.

2 Layer the backing, batting, and quilt top. Baste the three layers together using your preferred method.

3 Quilt as desired. I quilted an allover design of—what else?—rainbows.

4 Referring to "Binding a Quilt" on page 77, bind your quilt using the 2½"-wide strips.

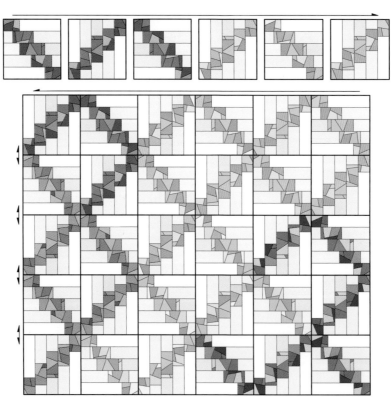

Quilt assembly

"Bitty Bits," designed and made by Melissa Corry.
Fabrics are Sunset and Sandcastle Kona collections for Robert Kaufman Fabrics.

Tiny triangles—or bitty bits—pieced onto block corners in an improvisational manner create the chain in this quilt. A scrappy background adds an extra pop to the design. This bed-sized stunner starts out with 5" squares, making it charm-square friendly and super quick to put together.

Finished quilt:
90½" x 90½", queen size

Finished block:
22½" x 22½"

Materials

Yardage is based on 42"-wide fabric.

7⅝ yards *total* of assorted light-neutral solids for blocks

3 yards *total* of assorted blue, green, and purple solids for blocks

⅞ yard of fabric for binding

8⅓ yards of fabric for backing

100" x 100" piece of batting

Cutting

From the assorted blue, green, and purple solids, cut a *total* of:

160 squares, 5" x 5"; cut in half diagonally to yield 320 triangles

From the assorted light-neutral solids, cut:

400 squares, 5" x 5"

From the binding fabric, cut:

10 strips, 2½" x 42"

Using Precuts

"Bitty Bits" is made entirely of 5" squares, so if you want to really speed up the cutting, just grab 4 charm packs of assorted solid colors and 10 charm packs of light solids for the background. The only cutting you have to do is halving the colored squares into triangles. Then you'll be ready to sew. Of course, you can always use prints instead of solids for a different look.

Piecing the A Blocks

1 Place a triangle on a corner of a light 5" square with right sides together as shown. Sew ¼" from the long edge of the triangle, and then trim along the triangle edge. Press the seam allowances toward the triangle.

2 Align the 5" lines of a square ruler with the corners of the light square and trim the unit to 5" x 5" square to make block A. Make 192 blocks, playing with the angle of the triangle to create variations in the corners.

Block A.
Make 192.

Varying Angles

The more you adjust the angles, the more variation you'll have in your finished quilt. Before you sew, hold a finger along the edge of the triangle and flip it back to ensure that it will extend past the edge of the background square. You'll quickly get the hang of how far you can vary the angles, but you can always do this little test first to double-check.

Piecing the B Blocks

1 Place a triangle on a corner of a light 5" square with right sides together as you did for block A. Sew ¼" from the long edge of the triangle, and then trim along the triangle edge. Press the seam allowances toward the triangle.

2 Place a second triangle on an adjacent corner of the light square with right sides together as shown. Sew ¼" from the long edge of the triangle, and then trim along the triangle edge. Press the seam allowances toward the triangle just added.

3 Align the 5" lines of a square ruler with the top, unpieced corners of the light square. Trim two sides of the block and then rotate the ruler to trim the third side so that the block measures 5" x 5". Make 64 of block B, varying the angles of the triangles.

Block B.
Make 64.

Piecing the AB Blocks

1 Lay out two light 5" squares, two A blocks, and one B block in a row. Sew the pieces together. Press the seam allowances to the right. Make 32 rows.

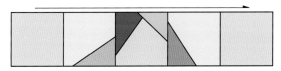

Make 32.

The Details

The scrappy background really is this quilt's "wow" factor, but feel free to make it your own. You don't have to stick with solids; a combination of several light prints, as in "End of the Rainbow" (page 51), would make a fabulous background. And who says you have to stick to light colors? I already want to make this quilt using light prints for the bitty bits and a mixture of dark prints for the background. The options are endless, so have some fun and make whatever you dream up.

2 Lay out one light 5" square and four A blocks in a row, rotating the A blocks as shown. Sew the pieces together. Press the seam allowances to the left. Make 32 rows.

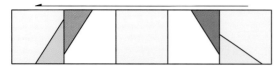

Make 32.

3 Lay out three light 5" squares and two B blocks in a row as shown. Sew the pieces together. Press the seam allowances to the right. Make 16 rows.

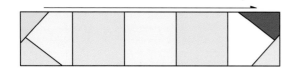

Make 16.

4 Lay out two rows from step 1, two rows from step 2, and one row from step 3 as shown. Pin and sew the rows together. Press the seam allowances open. Make 16 of block AB.

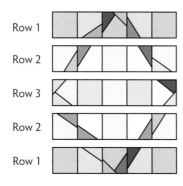

Row 1
Row 2
Row 3
Row 2
Row 1

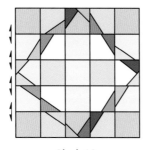

Block AB.
Make 16.

Assembling the Quilt Top

1 Lay out the AB blocks in four rows with four blocks per row as shown in the assembly diagram below.

2 Pin and sew the blocks into rows. Press the seam allowances in opposite directions from row to row.

3 Pin and sew the rows together, finishing the quilt top. Press the seam allowances open.

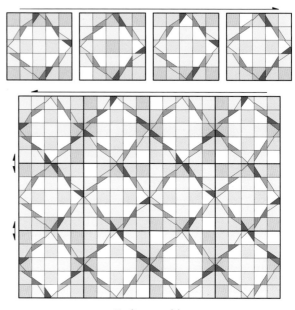

Quilt assembly

Finishing the Quilt

1 Cut the backing fabric into three 100"-long pieces. Remove the selvages and sew the three pieces together using a ½" seam allowance; press the seam allowances to one side. Trim the backing to approximately 100" x 100".

2 Layer the backing, batting, and quilt top. Baste the three layers together using your preferred method.

3 Quilt as desired. I used parallel straight lines ¼" apart in the triangles and echo quilted paisleys in the background.

4 Referring to "Binding a Quilt" on page 77, bind your quilt using the 2½"-wide strips.

Appliquéd Chains

Appliqué allows you to use any shape in a quilt, expanding design options to include not just straight and gently curved lines, but anything you can imagine. Appliqué is a fabulous design tool that's often passed over with the assumption that it's too hard. But if you can piece, you can appliqué! Give it a try, and before long, you'll want to add a bit of appliqué flair to every project.

Daisy Chain

"Daisy Chain," designed and made by Melissa Corry.
Fabrics are True Colors by Anna Maria Horner for Free Spirit Fabrics.

When my mother was a child in England, she used to sit in the fields for hours making daisy-chain necklaces, bracelets, and headbands. Since my mother played a big role in the original inspiration for this book, it seemed only fitting to create a design based on one of her childhood memories.

Finished quilt: 44½" x 44½", baby size

Finished block: 11" x 11"

Materials

Yardage is based on 42"-wide fabric.

2⅛ yards of white solid for block backgrounds

¾ yard *total* of assorted purple and pink prints for petal appliqués

½ yard of green print for stem and leaf appliqués

¼ yard of yellow print for flower-center appliqués

½ yard of fabric for binding

2⅓ yards of fabric for backing

54" x 54" piece of batting

3¼ yards of 18"-wide lightweight fusible web

Cutting

From the white solid, cut:
16 squares, 11½" x 11½"

From the binding fabric, cut:
5 strips, 2½" x 42"

Petal Note

If you want the petals of each flower to be made from the same print, as in the quilt shown, you'll need to cut five sets of four matching petals, four sets of two matching petals, and four petals for the corners. Refer to the quilt assembly diagram on page 62 for guidance and plan the placement of the flowers and blocks before you appliqué the pieces to the background. If you prefer flowers with a scrappy look, cut and lay out your petal appliqués randomly.

Adding the Appliqué

1 Referring to "Appliqué Basics" on page 76, prepare and cut 32 petals, 32 flower centers, 16 stems, and 32 leaves using the patterns on page 63. Read "Petal Note," below left, before cutting the petals.

2 Arrange two petal appliqués in opposite corners of a white 11½" square, aligning the edges. Arrange two flower-center appliqués next to the petal appliqués, aligning the straight edges with the edges of the background block. Position a stem appliqué diagonally as shown, sliding the ends of the stem under the edges of the petals. Arrange two leaf appliqués, one on each side of the stem.

3 Fuse the appliqués in place following the manufacturer's instructions. Stitch around each appliqué shape; I used a blanket stitch. Make 16 blocks.

Make 16.

The Details

If you want to quilt a floral design in the center of your chains the way I have, a disappearing-ink pen will really help. It can be hard to free-motion stitch such a large design without any markings. So grab a blue or purple pen—such as a Frixon, Sew Line, or The Fine Line—and draw in the flower center, using the seam lines as a guide. Then add a few petals around the center. When you're actually stitching, you can add in the details. When finished, spritz with water and you are left with a beautiful design to complement your chain.

Assembling the Quilt Top

1 Lay out the blocks in four rows with four blocks per row, rotating the blocks as shown in the assembly diagram above right.

2 Pin and sew the blocks into rows. Press the seam allowances open.

3 Pin and sew the rows together, finishing the quilt top. Press the seam allowances open.

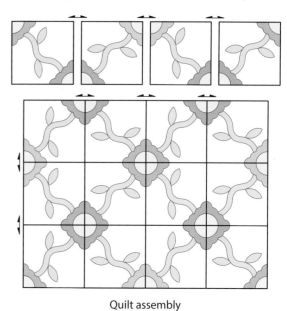

Quilt assembly

Finishing the Quilt

1 Cut the backing fabric into one 54"-long piece and a 28"-long piece. Remove the selvages. Cut the 28" piece into two 28" x 21" pieces and sew them together along the 21" edges using a ½" seam allowance. Press the seam allowances to one side. Sew this piece to the 54"-long piece along the 54" edges using a ½" seam allowance; press the seam allowances to one side. Trim the backing to approximately 54" x 54".

2 Layer the backing, batting, and quilt top. Baste the three layers together using your preferred method.

3 Quilt as desired. I quilted miniature loops in the print flowers, and I added a flower design with a traveling curl in the background.

4 Referring to "Binding a Quilt" on page 77, bind your quilt using the 2½"-wide strips.

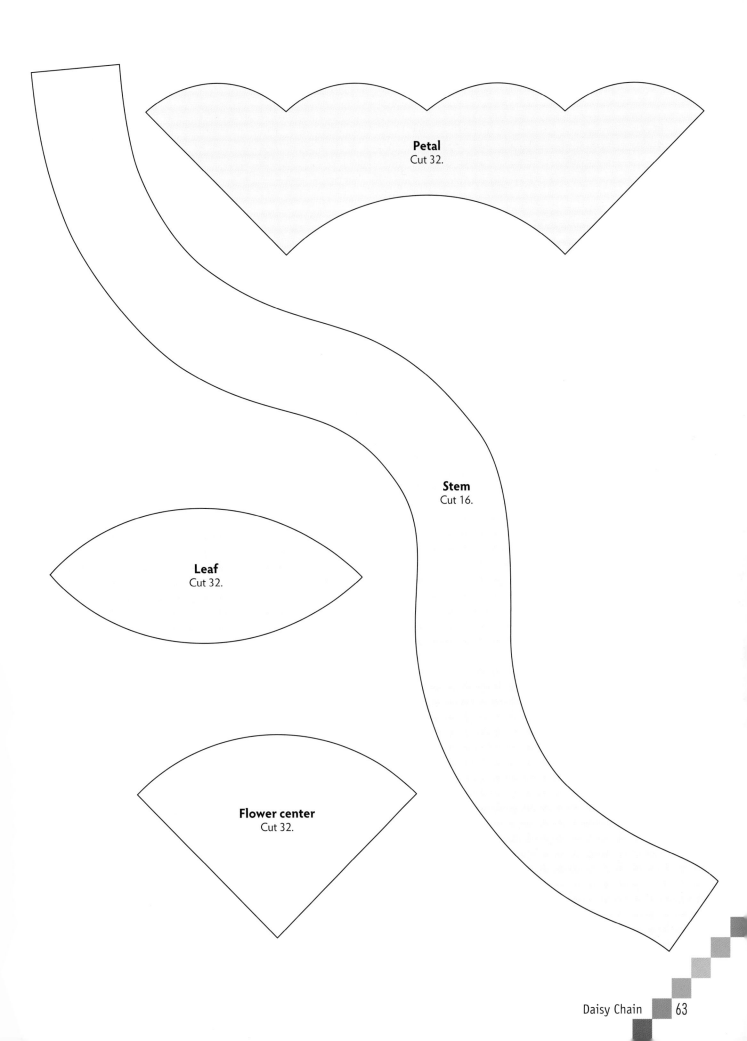

Petal
Cut 32.

Stem
Cut 16.

Leaf
Cut 32.

Flower center
Cut 32.

The Village Square

"The Village Square," designed and made by Melissa Corry.
Fabrics are Sidewalks by October Afternoon for Riley Blake Designs.

Quaint little houses and cornerstone blocks populate this Irish Chain design. I love the way each nine-patch unit makes a gathering place in the center of the village square. This village is great fun to put together, and you just can't help but smile at each of those sweet little dwellings.

Finished quilt:
83" x 83",
full size

Finished block:
12" x 12"

Materials

Yardage is based on 42"-wide fabric.

6¾ yards of white solid for block backgrounds and sashing

1⅔ yards *total* of assorted prints for blocks and appliqués

¼ yard of red print for sashing squares*

¾ yard of fabric for binding*

7¾ yards of fabric for backing

93" x 93" piece of batting

2¾ yards of 18"-wide lightweight fusible web (optional)

If you wish to bind the quilt with the same red print used for sashing squares, as in the quilt shown, you'll need a total of 1 yard.

Cutting

From the assorted prints, cut:
  108 squares, 2½" x 2½"

From the white solid, cut:
  18 strips, 5½" x 42"; crosscut into 72 rectangles, 5½" x 8½"
  28 strips, 2" x 42"; crosscut into 84 rectangles, 2" x 12½"
  27 strips, 2½" x 42"; crosscut into:
    72 rectangles, 2½" x 10½"
    72 rectangles, 2½" x 3½"

From the red print, cut:
  3 strips, 2" x 42"; crosscut into 49 squares, 2" x 2"

From the binding fabric, cut:
  9 strips, 2½" x 42"

Add Variety
With lots of small pieces, this quilt will help you clean out your scrap basket and use up precuts. The more colors and prints, the more charming your village will be!

Piecing the Blocks

1 Sew a print 2½" square and a white 2½" x 10½" rectangle together. Press the seam allowances toward the print square. Make 72 top/bottom rows.

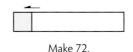

Make 72.

2 Sew two white 2½" x 3½" rectangles to opposite sides of a print 2½" square. Press the seam allowances toward the print square. Make 36 center units.

Make 36.

3 Sew a white 5½" x 8½" rectangle to each long side of a center unit. Press the seam allowances toward the white rectangles. Make 36 center rows.

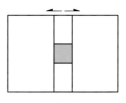

Make 36.

4 Lay out and sew two top/bottom rows and one center row together as shown. Press the seam allowances away from the center. Make 18 of block A.

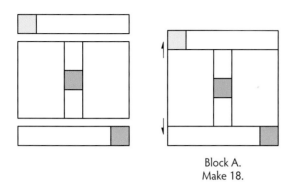

Block A.
Make 18.

5 Lay out and sew two top/bottom rows and one center row together as shown. Press the seam allowances away from the center. Make 18 of block B.

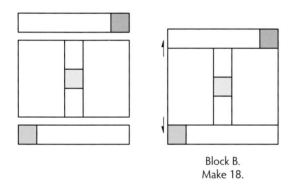

Block B.
Make 18.

Adding the Appliqué

Because I wanted my appliqué shapes to have scruffy, frayed raw edges, I didn't use fusible web for this project. I simply pinned the houses, doors, and roofs in place until I was ready to stitch them into position. This is an option to consider; you can use fusible web if you prefer. Refer to "Appliqué Basics" on page 76 if you plan to use fusible web, and draw the squares and rectangles onto the paper side of the fusible web.

1 Prepare and cut the following shapes from the assorted prints for the appliqués.

18 squares, 3½" x 3½", for houses

18 rectangles, 3" x 3½", for houses

18 squares, 3" x 3", for houses

18 rectangles, 2½" x 3", for houses

72 rectangles, 1" x 1½", for doors

4 rectangles, 4" x 4½"; cut into quarters diagonally to make 16 triangles for roofs

5 squares, 4" x 4"; cut into quarters diagonally to make 20 triangles for roofs

4 rectangles, 3½" x 4"; cut into quarters diagonally to make 16 triangles for roofs

5 squares, 3½" x 3½"; cut into quarters diagonally to make 20 triangles for roofs

---

Stabilize with Starch

If you're not appliquéing with fusible web, use a good-quality spray starch on the appliqué fabrics before cutting. The starch will give the fabrics a bit more body and make them easy to stitch in place. You'll need to launder your quilt when it's finished to remove the starch.

---

2 Arrange two house appliqués and two roof appliqués on an A block as shown. Position a door appliqué on each house.

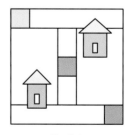

Block A

3 Pin the appliqués in position or, if using fusible web, fuse in place following the manufacturer's instructions. Stitch around each appliqué shape. I used a straight stitch ⅛" from the edges of each appliqué. Repeat to appliqué all 18 of the A blocks.

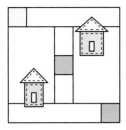

Block A

4 Arrange two house appliqués and two roof appliqués on a B block as shown. Position a door appliqué on each house. Repeat step 3 to appliqué all 18 of the B blocks.

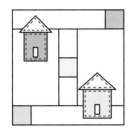

Block B

Making a Village

When arranging the appliqués on the blocks, feel free to play with the placement. The houses can be oriented any way you like. Just be sure to leave a ¼" seam allowance on the edges of your blocks free from appliqué. Add different-sized roofs to different-sized houses. Make this village your own original creation.

The Details

When arranging the appliqués on the blocks, feel free to play with the placement. The houses can be oriented any way you like, moving them up, down, or side to side. This adds some fun randomness to your chain. Just be sure to leave a ¼" seam allowance on the edges of your blocks. To add more randomness, don't be afraid to mix up the roof and house pairings and orientations. Add different-sized roofs to different-sized houses. And place some of the rectangle houses horizontally and some vertically. All of these small alterations will make the village your own original creation.

Assembling the Quilt Top

1 Lay out the A and B blocks in six rows with six blocks per row, alternating the block placement as shown in the assembly diagram below. Add the white 2" x 12½" rectangles and red 2" squares around the blocks to create the sashing.

2 Sew the sashing rectangles and sashing squares into rows. Press the seam allowances toward the sashing rectangles. Pin and sew the sashing rectangles and blocks into rows. Press the seam allowances toward the sashing rectangles.

3 Pin and sew the rows together, finishing the quilt top. Press the seam allowances open.

Finishing the Quilt

1 Cut the backing fabric into three 93"-long pieces. Remove the selvages and sew the three pieces together using a ½" seam allowance; press the seam allowances to one side. Trim the backing to approximately 93" x 93".

2 Layer the backing, batting, and quilt top. Baste the three layers together using your preferred method.

3 Quilt as desired. I quilted allover cobblestones in the background.

4 Referring to "Binding a Quilt" on page 77, bind your quilt using the 2½"-wide strips.

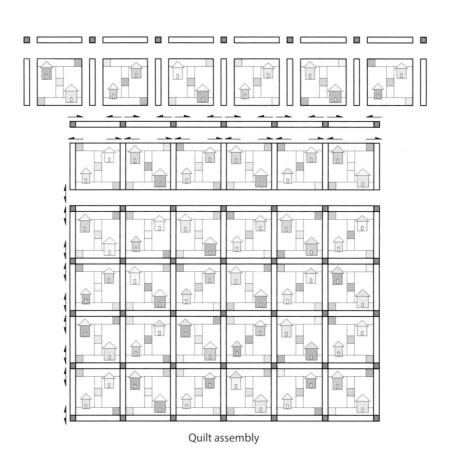

Quilt assembly

"Connect the Dots," designed and made by Melissa Corry.
Fabrics are Sunrise Kona collection for Robert Kaufman Fabrics.

I love polka dots, so I couldn't resist creating a chain that's practically a polka-dot profusion. Adding quarter circles in the corners creates a jolt, as four colors come together in one small-but-mighty multicolored polka dot. All in all, this is simply a super-fun quilt!

Finished quilt:
92½" x 92½",
queen size

Finished block:
11½" x 11½"

Materials

Yardage is based on 42"-wide fabric.

8 yards of white solid for block backgrounds

2⅛ yards *total* of assorted solids for appliqués

⅞ yard of fabric for binding

8⅝ yards of fabric for backing

102" x 102" piece of batting

4¼ yards of 18"-wide lightweight fusible web

Cutting

From the white solid, cut:
64 squares, 12" x 12"

From the binding fabric, cut:
10 strips, 2½" x 42"

Adding the Appliqué

1 Referring to "Appliqué Basics" on page 76, prepare 64 small circles, 128 medium circles, and 32 large circles using the patterns on page 72 and the assorted solid fabrics. Cut the large circles into quarters for a total of 128 quarter circles.

2 Fold a white 12" square in half diagonally and finger-press the fold to create a placement guide.

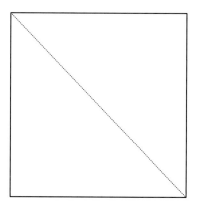

3 Arrange two quarter circles, two medium circles, and one small circle along the finger-pressed line. Align the straight sides of the quarter circles with the corners of the background block, and center the three remaining circles along the line as shown.

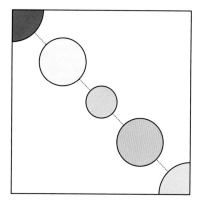

4 Fuse the appliqué shapes in place following the manufacturer's instructions. Stitch around each circle; I used a tight zigzag stitch.

5 Repeat steps 2–4 to make 64 blocks.

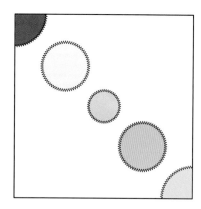

Make 64.

Assembling the Quilt Top

1 Lay out the blocks in eight rows with eight blocks per row, rotating the blocks as shown in the assembly diagram below.

2 Pin and sew the blocks into rows. Press the seam allowances open.

3 Pin and sew the rows together, finishing the quilt top. Press the seam allowances open.

Connecting the Chain

When sewing the blocks together, take care to match the quarter circles so that your multicolored dot forms a nice, smooth circle. It's easy to see the edges of your appliqué, thanks to the precise stitching.

Finishing the Quilt

1 Cut the backing fabric into three 103"-long pieces. Remove the selvages and sew the three pieces together using a ½" seam allowance; press the seam allowances to one side. Trim the backing to approximately 103" x 103".

2 Layer the backing, batting, and quilt top. Baste the three layers together using your preferred method.

The Details

Quilting this project with dense pebbling in the background and no quilting on the appliqué creates a faux trapunto look. The dots pop up a bit, making it look like I added extra batting behind them, but it's simply due to the lack of quilting on them. If you don't like that look, you can always quilt right over the appliqués. I think quilting little swirls would be super fun, adding spiral designs in the polka dots.

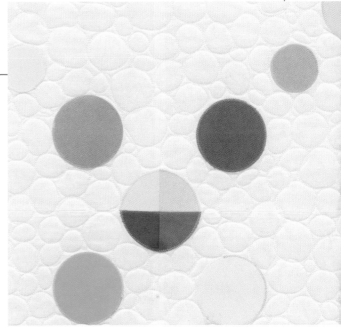

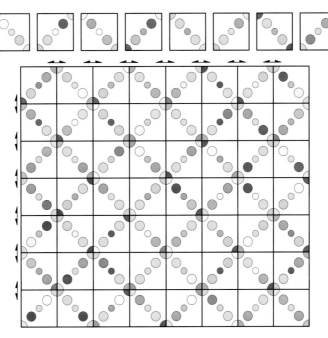

Quilt assembly

3 Quilt as desired. I quilted pebbles of varying sizes in the background and left the circles unquilted so they would really stand out.

4 Referring to "Binding a Quilt" on page 77, bind your quilt using the 2½"-wide strips.

"Binding a Quilt" on page 77

Scrappy Binding

I had leftover strips from each of the solid colors and decided to add a fun scrappy binding to finish this quilt. The binding concept reflects a sunrise: I used green along the bottom to represent grass, and then I moved to glowing hues of yellow and orange along the sides and finally into the brilliant pinks and reds at the top.

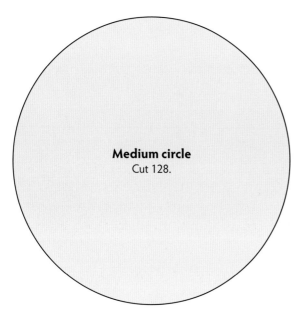

Medium circle
Cut 128.

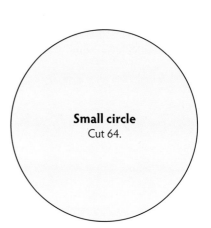

Small circle
Cut 64.

Cutting line

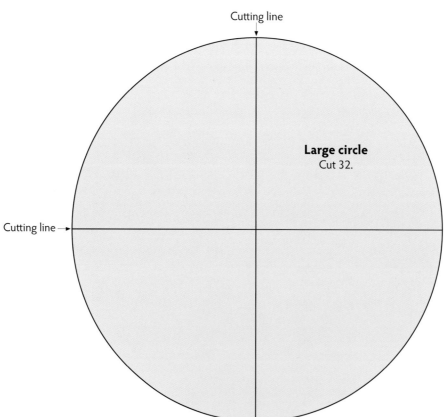

Large circle
Cut 32.

Cutting line →

Quiltmaking Basics

If you are new to quilting, many of the processes may seem rather daunting at first and there is a lot to take in. There isn't space to cover everything within these pages, and many books are available for beginning quilters. Most quilt shops offer classes and always welcome new quilters. In addition, I have created several tutorials that explain many of the techniques used in these projects, including appliqué basics, crazy-patch piecing, basting, quilting, and binding. You can find these how-tos at my blog, www.HappyQuiltingMelissa.com. Martingale also has a website, ShopMartingale.com/HowtoQuilt, with lots of free information on rotary cutting, piecing, and other basic quiltmaking techniques. There is a wealth of instruction in print and online to help guide you along your quilting journey.

Accuracy

Accuracy in quiltmaking is essential, playing a vital role in three main areas: cutting, piecing, and pressing.

Cutting. Cut fabrics using a rotary cutter, cutting mat, and a quilting ruler. Press the fabric before cutting to remove wrinkles.

Piecing. Sewing a straight and accurate ¼" seam allowance is vital. If you have a ¼" presser foot for your sewing machine, your life will be a lot easier, because you can simply align your pieces with the edge of the foot. To double-check the accuracy of your ¼" seam allowance, sew a few seams and use a quilting ruler to measure the width of your seam allowance. The stitching should be right along the ¼" mark on your ruler.

Pins are your friends. If I have a seam that has to be aligned, a long strip to sew, or blocks to stitch together, I pin them before sewing. Insert the pin with the head lying on the fabric that will be on top when you sew, allowing you to easily pull out the pin with your left hand just before the pin reaches the needle. Avoid sewing over pins; they're not your needle's friends.

Now, I'm not saying that every point in every quilt I make is just perfect. Quilting is supposed to be fun. If your points aren't absolutely flawless or your seams don't align precisely, it's OK. Move on and continue to grow and learn.

Pressing. Although often overlooked, pressing is a vastly important step. Take the time to accurately and gently press each unit after it is sewn. This will help you achieve accurate piecing and will also ensure that your quilt top lies flat when it is finished. Pressing is different from ironing. Ironing uses a back-and-forth motion that can easily stretch your pieces; pressing involves an up-and-down motion that helps avoid stretching.

The step-by-step instructions with each project indicate my recommendations for pressing seam allowances. The pressing directions allow seams to "nest" whenever possible. Nesting occurs when two seams are aligned and the seam allowances are pressed in opposing directions. This allows them to lock and makes sewing accurate seam allowances much easier. In some cases, I press the seam allowances open. This is to avoid bulk where many seams come together. Feel free to press to one side if you prefer.

Nesting seam allowances

Strip Piecing

Strip piecing is a great timesaving technique. Rather than cutting and sewing individual squares, you'll sew strips together first to create a strip set, and then cut the strip set into segments. This saves time and thread and is very accurate. When strip piecing, shorten your stitch length to ensure that stitching will be secure after cutting.

1 Sew strips together along the edges, aligning them as you stitch. If the ends of the strip don't line up exactly, it won't matter. You'll trim the ends before subcutting. Press as directed.

2 Lay the strip set on your cutting mat horizontally. Align a ruler with the edges and seam. Trim the selvage end using your rotary cutter to create a straight edge.

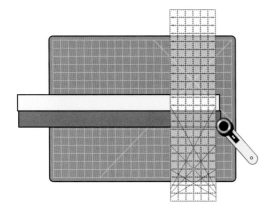

3 Rotate the strip 180° and, starting from the newly cut end, measure one segment width as specified in your project's instructions; cut along the edge of the ruler. Continue until you have the desired number of strip-pieced segments. You may need to straighten the edge of the strip set again after three or four cuts.

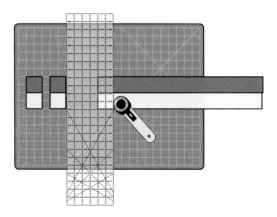

4 If you need to cut multiple strip sets, lay them out on your cutting mat, one above the other. Use the horizontal and vertical lines on the cutting mat to align them, and measure with your ruler to subcut them. Be very careful when cutting this way or your results may not be as accurate as if using just the ruler to measure.

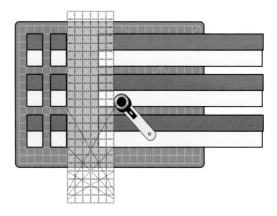

Crazy-Patch Piecing

Crazy-patch piecing is a great way to use up those scraps that seem to take over your sewing space. And it's so much fun because there are no rules—you can truly piece in any direction you like. There are several methods of crazy piecing, but this is the way I like to do it.

1 Sew two scraps together along whichever edges align the best. Press seam allowances to one side, usually toward the darker fabric.

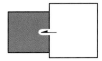

2 Using a ruler and rotary cutter, trim a straight edge along any side of the pieced scraps. Sew a scrap to the newly created straight edge. Press seam allowances to one side.

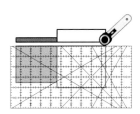
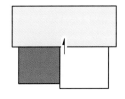

3 Continue in this fashion, adding scraps until your block reaches the desired dimensions. Try to keep the scraps roughly the same size. This means that as your block gets larger, you'll need to piece scraps together first and then create a straight edge along one side of the pieced scraps. Add the pieced scraps to the straight edge of your original unit.

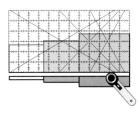
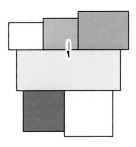

4 You don't have to work solely in squares and rectangles. When trimming straight edges, you can trim at angles, however sharp you like. You can also trim a fifth or even a sixth side at a wild

angle. This allows you to add those triangle scraps that you don't know what to do with, and it will make your piecing crazier at the same time.

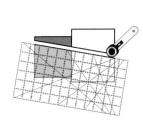
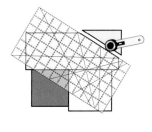

Trimming Blocks at an Angle

For improvisational piecing, you'll sometimes be directed to trim blocks at an angle. This gives the block a slightly askew, "wonky" look. It isn't much different from trimming a block to be square, but it's a whole lot more fun. When trimming, play with the angle of the ruler and observe the different looks you can achieve.

1 Place your block on a cutting mat. If you have a square ruler that is the exact size to which you are trimming your block, simply place the ruler on the block at an angle. Ensure that every edge of the ruler remains on the block, although corners can touch the edges of the block. Trim around all four sides of the ruler to create your new angled block.

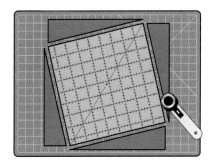

2 If your square ruler is larger than the size needed, place the ruler on the block at an angle. Ensure that the top and right edges of the ruler are completely on the block; also check the ruler markings of the desired trimming size to ensure that they remain on the block as well. Trim the right and top edges of the block.

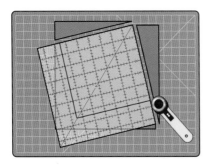

3 Rotate the block 180° and align the desired measurements on your ruler with the two edges you just trimmed. Trim the remaining two edges to create your angled block.

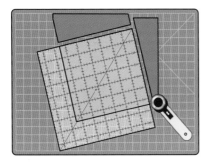

Appliqué Basics

The appliqué quilts in this book use a raw-edge appliqué technique that's both fun and easy. If you've never tried appliqué, don't worry. There are just a few basic steps to learn.

Start with fusible web. (I use Wonder Under or HeatNBond most often.) As you don't want your appliqué to be super stiff, always look for the lightweight or "lite" product.

1 With a pencil or permanent marker, trace the desired number of patterns onto the paper side of the fusible web, leaving about ½" between shapes. Roughly cut out the traced appliqué shapes, leaving about ¼" around the drawn lines.

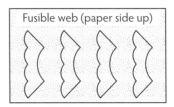

Fusible web (paper side up)

2 Following the manufacturer's directions, fuse the non-paper side of the web to the wrong side of your appliqué fabric. And trust me, if it says to press with a dry iron, you want to use a dry iron. Otherwise, removing that paper is a real pain. I know from experience. After fusing, allow the piece to cool.

3 Cut the appliqué pieces along the drawn lines and remove the paper backing from the fusible web. Place an appliqué shape on your background block or strip and ensure that it is right where you want it. Then follow the manufacturer's directions to press the appliqué in place, fusing it into position. Remember to press with an up-and-down motion, not a side-to-side motion that could shift the appliqué.

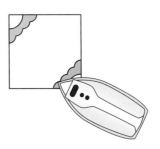

4 The final step is to stitch around the edges of your appliqué shapes. You can use any stitch you like. Just be sure to go around all of the raw edges of your appliqué. I generally use a blanket stitch, a zigzag stitch, or a straight stitch $\frac{1}{8}$" from the edges of the appliqués.

Blanket stitch   Narrow zigzag stitch   Straight stitch

Basting a Quilt

Press the quilt top one last time to make sure that seam allowances are flat and there are no wrinkles. Prepare the backing as directed in the project instructions. You can always create a scrappy backing to use up random or leftover pieces of fabric. Just press it well and ensure that it is 6" to 10" larger than your quilt top, allowing 3" to 5" extra on each side.

I usually baste with safety pins or basting spray. Safety pins are extremely cost-effective, as you can use them over and over. Spray basting is extremely time efficient but can be a little costly. Layer the backing, batting, and quilt top and space pins about a hand's width apart. Follow the manufacturer's instructions when using basting spray to prevent sticky residue in the surrounding area and to ensure adequate ventilation.

Machine Quilting

I know it sounds scary, but trust me: machine quilting is tons of fun once you get the hang of it. You will need to read your user's manual to figure out how your sewing machine works with free-motion quilting, and of course you will need to practice. But just give it some time, and before long you will love it.

To machine quilt, you will need a walking foot and a darning foot. A walking foot allows you to quilt straight lines easily. The feed dogs on the bottom of the foot will push the quilting

sandwich through your machine evenly. A darning foot allows you to stitch a free-motion design by moving the fabric. I like to practice my design on paper first and then move to my quilt top.

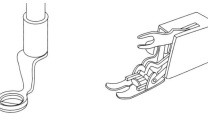

Darning foot   Walking foot attachment

Binding a Quilt

Binding is the finishing touch on your quilt and can be applied by hand or machine. Hand binding gives a beautiful finished look with hidden threads. Machine binding leaves a stitch line on the binding, but it's fast and very strong. I use both methods depending on the intended use of the quilt and the recipient. If attaching the binding by machine, use a walking foot if you have one; it will move the layers evenly as you sew.

1 Cut the number of binding strips specified in the project instructions. I always use 2½"-wide strips for my binding.

2 Join the strips by placing them at a 90° angle with right sides together. Sew a diagonal seam from corner to corner. For greater accuracy, mark the diagonal line first and then sew on the line. Trim the excess fabric ¼" from the stitching and press the seam allowances open so the binding strip lies flat.

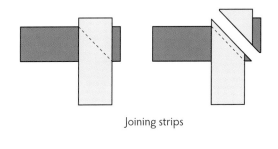

Joining strips

Press seam allowances open.

3 Fold the binding strip in half with wrong sides together and press.

4 Starting in the center of one side of the quilt, align the raw edges of the quilt and the binding. I align the strip with the edge of my quilt as I go and don't use pins, but you can pin if you like. If you are hand sewing the binding, you will attach the binding to the front of your quilt; if you are finishing by machine, you will attach the binding to the back of your quilt.

5 Leave 10" of the binding strip loose and begin sewing using a ¼" seam allowance along the edge, backstitching at the start. Continue stitching until you are ¼" from the corner of the quilt; stop stitching with your needle down. Rotate the quilt 90° and backstitch off the edge of the quilt, creating a small L shape in the stitching. Remove the quilt from the machine.

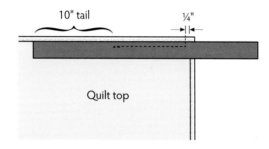

10" tail   ¼"

Quilt top

6 Fold the binding up and away from the quilt, creating a backward L shape with the binding strip. Fold the binding strip straight down so it is aligned with the next side of the quilt. Begin stitching ¼" from the edge of your quilt through the folded layers of binding. Backstitch a few

stitches and then continue stitching forward, aligning the raw edges of the binding strip with the edge of your quilt as you go.

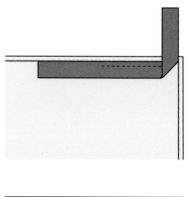

7 Continue stitching the binding to the quilt in this fashion until you are within 10" of the loose end of the binding strip. Lay the two loose ends on top of one another. Measure a 2½" overlap (the same as the width of the binding) and cut away the excess.

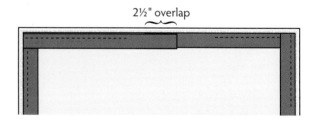

2½" overlap

8 Unfold the loose binding-strip ends and lay them with right sides together at a 90° angle. Pin and sew a diagonal seam from corner to corner, marking the diagonal line first if desired. Trim the excess fabric ¼" from the seam.

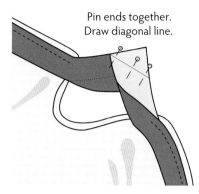

Pin ends together.
Draw diagonal line.

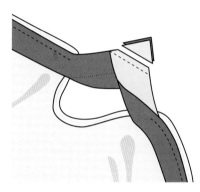

9 Refold the binding and finish sewing the binding to the quilt. Backstitch a few stitches at the beginning and the end.

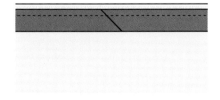

10 If you are hand stitching your binding, use a blind stitch to secure the edge of the binding to the back of the quilt, covering the seam line with the folded edge of the binding. If you are machine stitching, use a straight, zigzag, or wavy stitch to secure the binding to the front of the quilt, covering the seam line with the folded edge of the binding. With either method, miter the corners as you get to them and stitch them in place.

About the Author

Melissa Corry began quilting in 2002. Her mother taught her the basics so she would have something to do in the evenings while her husband was studying in medical school. She enjoyed making baby quilts for friends and family and even the occasional bed quilt. In 2010, Melissa created her blog, Happy Quilting, and her hobby quickly became a passion.

Melissa loves all things quilting, from designing to binding and everything in between. Quilting is a creative respite for her, and as a busy mom of five little ones, she often says, "It is the one thing I do in my day that stays done." In short, quilting makes her happy, and she loves to share that joy of quilting with others.

Since joining the online community of quilters, Melissa has started her own pattern line, her quilts have been published in several prominent magazines, and she has shared her projects in five collaborative books. This is her first solo publication, an amazing dream come true. To see more of Melissa's daily quilting adventures, visit her website at www.HappyQuiltingMelissa.com.

Acknowledgments

This book would not have been possible without the help and support of my family and wonderful people within this incredible industry. Special thanks go to:

My family: my husband, Jacob, and my children, Spencer, Jessica, Kristian, Kamryn, and Jocelyn, for your patience, support, encouragement, and love. Mommy loves you so much!

My amazing mother-in-law, Barbara, for countless hours of hand binding each and every quilt in this book, for letting me "hog" your long-arm machine, and for always being there to offer advice, help in a pinch, and give encouragement every step of the way.

My mother, Christine, who instilled this love of quilting within me, for being my sounding board, for having endless phone chats over this design or that color, and for always believing in me.

Art Gallery Fabrics for providing the beautiful fabrics featured in "The North Star" and "Coins in the Fountain."

Free Spirit Fabrics for providing the beautiful fabrics featured in "Unraveled," "Charm Bracelet," and "Daisy Chain."

Moda for providing the beautiful fabrics featured in "Two Paths Crossed," "An Irish Braid," "String of Pearls," and "Fractured."

Riley Blake Designs for providing the beautiful fabrics featured in "Breaking Up" and "The Village Square."

Robert Kaufman Fabrics for providing the beautiful fabrics featured in "Pick Up Sticks," "Bitty Bits," and "Connect the Dots."

My fabulous Happy Quilting readers for daily encouragement. Your comments, emails, and pictures mean the world to me and are a constant reminder of why I love this industry and the extraordinary people in it.